Praise for
Treasure Found

"To navigate life's tumultuous terrain, we need courageous guides who have embarked on their own journey of self-discovery and are willing to delve into the uncharted terrain. In *Treasure Found* Faith Donaldson accomplishes just that by taking readers on an emotional journey into the dark and unfinished places of pain and hurt, only to emerge into a realm of profound self-discovery and empowerment.

"*Treasure Found* is not just a book—it is a road map for navigating life's challenges with honesty, grace, grit, resilience, and acceptance.

"With its wisdom and heartfelt storytelling, *Treasure Found* is essential reading for anyone seeking hope, healing, and redemption in the face of adversity. Faith Donaldson will guide you on a transformative journey to reclaim your own lost treasures, offering courage and grace as companions along the way."

—Brandon Addison
Coach and Story Guide
www.bacoach.co

"It is a rare gift for an author to share their journey in a way that helps you better understand your own. *Treasure Found* does exactly that. Faith Donaldson shares rich wisdom and inspiration unearthed from a lifetime of overcoming profound adversity, doing so in a way that invites you to share your story as well. Faith has personally helped me through some very difficult times by walking with me as a dear friend, and that same spirit is evident here. From the first page, you, too, will have that feeling of her arm in yours, and you'll finish the book feeling empowered and hopeful.

"This beautifully written book is authentic. Faith is not a superhero, but a fellow traveler who has had both victories and failures. She fearlessly shares both in a way that many will relate to. As a former educator and currently as a trauma-informed life coach, I will be sharing *Treasure Found* with the people I work with for years to come because it reaches the heart, not just the head."

—Allison Bown, CPLC, TICC
Author of *The Image* and *Grace Spaces*
Founder of Grace Spaces Training and Coaching
www.gracespaces.org

"*Treasure Found* is astute, accessible, and beautifully written. Faith Donaldson bridges a lifetime of complex trauma to the process of healing and resilience. A magnificent gift to survivors."

—Richard Audsley, PhD, LMFT
Marriage & Family Therapist

"My friend Faith has followed her calling to write *Treasure Found*, digging deep into her challenging life stories to unearth gems that speak to who she is and how she shows up today. Through it all, she reminds us there is power in every single story."

—Lois Melkonian, MCC
Executive and Mentor Coach
www.loismelkonian.com

"Beautifully written, *Treasure Found* is a compelling and riveting story that sweeps over the reader like a river of healing water, lending immeasurable hope and inspiration. Faith Donaldson holds nothing back as she shares her raw and transparent journey of how she navigated intolerable situations and inconceivable circumstances. Her courage, hard work, and great desire for healing turn horrendous defeat into glorious victory. With wisdom and guidance, she constructs a pathway toward healing, guiding the reader to confront their own emotional issues and inner wounds. She provides transformative and provocative practices within these pages to help the reader engage in their own journey.

"The book intertwines courage, struggle, spirituality, and triumph in a way that breathes life into the soul. It is an anthem of hope, fostering the beauty in transforming darkness into light."

—Sandi Gardner-Wood
Trauma Survivor

Treasure Found

Treasure Found

The Hidden Gems *in* *our* Life Experiences

FAITH DONALDSON

ILLUMIFY
MEDIA.COM

Treasure Found
Copyright © 2024 by Faith Donaldson

All rights reserved. No part of this book may be reproduced in any form or by any means—whether electronic, digital, mechanical, or otherwise—without permission in writing from the publisher, except by a reviewer, who may quote brief passages in a review.

The views and opinions expressed in this book are those of the author and do not necessarily reflect the official policy or position of llumify Media Global.

All scripture quotations, unless otherwise indicated, are taken from *The Message Version, The Bible in Contemporary Language,* by Eugene H. Peterson, Copyright © 2023, NavPress.

Published by
Illumify Media Global
www.IllumifyMedia.com
"Let's bring your book to life!"

Library of Congress Control Number: 2024908372

Paperback ISBN: 978-1-964251-01-1
Hardcover ISBN: 978-1-964251-02-8

Email the author at connecttofaithd@outlook.com

Cover design by Debbie Lewis

Printed in the United States of America

Dedication

I dedicate this book to
every determined seeker
every courageous explorer
every resilient overcomer
and every persistent believer who knows
there is yet more to life.
May you remain steadfast on your journey.

Contents

Prologue: The Mirror, Part I xiii
Introduction xxi
1 The Mirror, Part II 1
2 What Might Have Been 11
3 Secrets 27
4 The Destroyer, Part I: What Happened? 41
5 The Restorer 55
6 It Will Be Over Soon 63
7 Betrayed 77
8 The Betrayer 87
9 Early Morning Dip 103
10 Hit from All Sides 111
11 The Destroyer, Part II: The Long-Term Impact 129
12 Treasure Found 147
Final Word to My Readers 165
Acknowledgments 167
Special Acknowledgments 171
Further Resources 173
About the Author 179

Prologue

The Mirror, Part I

*"Everyone carries a shadow,
and the less it is embodied in the individual's conscious life,
the blacker and denser it is."*
—Carl Jung

Author's Note: *When facing a part of ourselves that we do not want to accept, no two experiences are the same. Some have more pleasant experiences in facing their shadow. "The Mirror" is my experience. Many will bypass this part of themselves altogether because they fear what they do not understand. To face our shadow is a choice we each decide to make or avoid. I can say from my own experience that the Shadow does not need to be feared, but rather, it should be valued for the truth it reveals.*

An ominous, explosive shiver runs from the base of my spine to the top of my neck. Then suddenly reversing, it exits out through my arms. I shake off this bodily current, while listening for the voice that created this reaction. *Will it speak to me again?*

I want to believe that there will be lasting silence from these beastly utterances, but intuitively, I think this unlikely. The voice has gotten louder with each passing day. Everything inside me wants to find an excuse to do something else—anything—but to sit in stillness. I feel it is a threat to my mind and soul. I tell myself I have a choice in this. *But do I?*

Slowly, I close my eyes. Before me, an image of myself approaches. The image is twisted, pained and fierce. She's dressed in a tattered black garment. Her hair is filled with grime and dirt, matted in chunks that would be impossible to smooth with a comb. There is a stench of ancient decay. The apparition draws nearer.

She holds a mirror in her hands, its glass facing me. Its rectangle is framed in scuffed tin, meant to be galvanized silver. It's a large mirror, and in it glimpses of my own image begin to appear.

I look nothing like her, I tell myself, not understanding what is unfolding before me.

This noxious figure now stands in front of me. I barely breathe as I attempt to keep my thinking clear with assurances that I am safe. I take a step back. Her eyes, blackened and biting, burrow into mine.

My instinct is to lower my eyes to disengage—but a wiser voice within warns that this would not be my best choice. Her piercing glare does not release me; my adrenaline heightens.

"What do you want?" I ask, my voice shaky and hesitant.

There is no response, only silence.

Attempting again to engage her, I ask, "Why have you been fighting me and screaming at me for two weeks?"

The Mirror, Part I

She takes a step back, lifting and thrusting the mirror into my face as she speaks. Her voice is stentorian, piercing, raging. She snarls, "Do you have the fucking courage to look into the mirror to see who you really are?"

I drop my head, turning to my right to break her loathsome stare. Her brusque voice reeks with hate and judgment; she's merciless.

Her glare intensifies. "Who the hell do you think you are? You have bathed yourself in light, but you have refused to see yourself for who you really are!"

Her words are meant to pierce me, and they do.

I abruptly interrupt, "Hold on! You do not have the right to define me! I don't have to accept your judgment."

She blasts back, spitting verbal venom, "Who the hell said anything about defining you? I said, 'Do you have the courage to look into the mirror to see who you really are?'—to face me, to face yourself?"

I feel my lungs catch a shallow breath; I hold it tightly, constricting the muscles in my chest, not knowing if I will be able to catch another. Finally, a release comes. I exhale. I wait.

My response to her question comes within a moment, but it feels like a thousand minutes.

"Okay, what do you want me to do, or to do to me?"

"Noooo!" she lashes back. "This has nothing to do with what I will do to you. It has everything to do with what you will do with me! How will you deal with me and face the truth that I hold?"

My anxiety rises. I don't want to believe that she holds any truth about me, but she is me and I am her. I do not know this part of myself. I do not *want* to know this part of myself.

With numbing hesitancy, I speak, trembling, "I feel that you have things to say to me about myself that I have not seen, and you are enraged that I have not embraced what you know."

She draws the mirror back from my face and, in a hard but less-overpowering voice, affirms, "I *do* have things to say to you. You have not wanted to hear what I know, but I hold what you have chosen to ignore—what you fear you will despise. I am you and you are me. Will you listen? Will you see?"

"Yes, I will listen," I reply. "I fear what you may say and show me, but I will listen without interrupting you."

She tells me, "Then sit, and let's begin."

I am surprised to suddenly find two chairs facing each other. We are outdoors in an unfamiliar space. It would be a beautiful place to explore, even safe, but with this mutated form in front of me, common sense tells me nothing is safe. Nevertheless, I sit. She sits across from me.

Slowly, she lifts the mirror again for me to see the image it reflects. "Look in the mirror. What do you see?"

"I see myself," I tell her.

"And who is that?" she asks.

I am silent. I know that I can tell her my true identity, but I fear that her rage will erupt once again. I sense she has something in mind, something she wants to tell me,

The Mirror, Part I

to reveal to me. I wonder why she doesn't just come out with it.

"I know who I am," I respond, "but I do not know who you are, and it appears that you hold a truth about me that I have not accepted. Perhaps a hidden part of me that has always felt and believed something dark about myself?"

She is still and relaxes a bit in her chair, but she continues to hold the mirror in front of me.

Taking a breath, she begins. "Look into the mirror and see—really see!"

I drop my eyes back to the image of myself. I look stressed and tired, fearful, yet seeking. I want this to be over—whatever this is, but my inner knower is fully aware that there is something for me to see and understand. I nod to give her permission to continue, mindful that she will decide when we begin.

I remain in my chair, staring into the mirror. Minutes pass in silence. Her voice has changed from its loud, demanding tone to one of factual authority. She does know something I do not know.

She begins, "Do you see the bitch in the mirror?"

Each of her words is a sword thrust into my reality. Her delivery is harsh, fierce: a bull's-eye to her target.

Her words are earsplitting. I want to shout back that this is not true, that I know who I am. I want to list all the ways that she is wrong. But I am here to listen. I bite more deeply into my tongue.

She gets on with it. "Do you know that you are a whore, a cruel and hateful liar? Do you know that you still withhold and guard yourself with fear? Do you know you are judgmental, accusatory, hidden—refusing to be seen in your vulnerability? Do you know that you refuse to be fully exposed? You take refuge in your true self-identity in the hope that no one will *ever* discover the ugliness that you fear others might see." She screams, "Look at yourself!"

I am shaken. My mind is spinning in the lostness of being confronted with what I have not believed. Yet somehow I am now beginning to see, dimly through this glass, that there may be truth in what she is saying to me. At the same time, I am confused, thinking of all the years it took me to overcome my negative beliefs about myself—to be able to finally see myself for who I really am, to believe that I am the person God saw me to be and about whom He said, "You are good."

Confusion spills over me like a tepid wave. I must keep my head on and think clearly. I need to understand that which I have not fully seen within myself—within this mirror.

She speaks again, "You have exiled me into a tidy box labeled 'Eliminated.' You cannot eliminate me just because you have come to see yourself in a new light. I am the part of you that you must come to understand. I am the layers of beliefs you carried as truths for most of your life!"

Fixing her stare on me, she continues. "Yes, you did process these beliefs, but you never untangled the complexity of how each stained you and how you carry them with you still. You don't have to accept at this moment that this is so, but you must come to understand that it is true. It is imperative that you see me for who I am and accept the truth that I offer, because *I cannot be who you are until you face who I am.*"

Introduction

Author's Note: *In the following chapters, names and identifying details of certain individuals have been changed to protect their privacy.*

The day's temperature is perfection. The sun warms my shoulders and melts the late spring snow that only yesterday blanketed the ground. *Finally, the hope of spring.* The warmth of summer will soon follow. My mind is clearer, my spirit is lighter than in winter. I have trekked through many such long, emotional winters. Today, I feel the freshness of new life that stretches out before me.

Lapsing into deep thought in my place in the sun on the deck, I lose all sense of time. Being in this moment is all that exists. My five senses are awakened and alive to what really matters in this one slice of significant reality. I sense this moment is a gift that somehow *is* for all time—as if this moment forever exists outside time.

The minutes slip by. I evaluate the thoughts gathering in my mind, reflecting on all that I have endured and overcome. My musings lead me to consider who I am as a person and where I now find myself.

I've gone far enough down this road of changing my life. I'm okay right where I am, one part of me wants to argue. *Has it been worth it to keep going all this time—to keep looking for what I somehow knew was still there to discover?*

These questions help sharpen my thoughts, which become clearer.

Perhaps the most challenging of all expeditions are not the ones that demand physical strength and training: reaching mountain summits, jumping from a plane with a parachute, being shot into space by 8.8 million pounds of thrust on NASA's rocket, or venturing into the blackness of uninvaded ocean depths.

Perhaps the most challenging of all expeditions are those that require the courage to look inward—to unlock that hidden safe, layered over with avoidance, in the hope that the secrets inside will never be discovered.

Perhaps the most challenging expedition is the choice to face the past. We can choose to ignore the past, believing that with time it will fade and disappear. But the truly valiant person is the one who courageously embarks on this inward journey.

The truly courageous are the ones who acknowledge the avoidance (even addictions) they created to silence the tormenting lies about themselves. They see that these lies have been embedded from their past experiences and still carry messages of blame, shame, and rejection. They are willing to confront these lies that resound within their mind today.

I smile, nodding to myself at my own conclusions. I deliberately chose to venture *inward* into the unknown. Many times, I doubted that I could gather the courage it would take to travel there. I calculate the length of time I have given to my journey—so many years. It has taken longer than I ever expected.

Introduction

For the first time, I am seeing something about myself: I will leave no stone unturned. I'm an emotional treasure hunter. Why did something happen? How have the events in my life affected me? What am I going to do about it? Where are my discoveries taking me?

This spring day in 2022 that I've just described launched me into the journey I am currently documenting. Today, I sit at my computer, aware that when I began writing *Treasure Found*, I was still unsure if I could claim my story as my own. Writing my story has freed me from many of the intrusive lies that were hanging around in my mind. With its completion, I now enter a new phase of my adventure.

This book, *Treasure Found*, holds my story, told in short segments of my journey. To write the entirety of what I have faced in life would be unnecessarily long. My story evolved in phases, which is likely the case for all of us.

When I began to tell others about the painful events of my life and all that has happened to me—including the destructive choices I made—it required that I risk rejection and judgment. This risk aroused a grip of inner terror that was overwhelming at times.

I remember a session like this with my very first therapist. In that meeting, I came to realize that there was intense fear lurking within me. I told him, "There is something undefined inside me, and I don't know what it is."

His response was, "Well then, we need to look inside."

In horror, I proclaimed, "We can't! If we go there, all we will find is a rotting corpse—a blackened mummy—a nothing."

He leaned slowly back in his chair. In his ever-so-kind and gentle voice he replied, "I believe we will find much more than that."

That was the beginning—day one of setting off on my expedition.

Six years later found me with a second therapist who would continue the journey with me. We worked through the normal issues that can arise in life, and I faced them head-on. I was moving into the final phase of terminating my therapy when my husband thought it would be a good idea to visit the town where I'd spent some years growing up.

On that visit, I wanted to see a certain farmhouse that I remembered. I especially felt that the back door of that house held something significant for me. I had no idea that when my eyes fell on that back door, I would experience my first full-blown panic attack. (I tell this story in more detail in Chapter 4, "The Destroyer, Part I: What Happened?")

When I was finally able to calm myself, I called my therapist to explain what had happened. His response was, "It's clear that we need to go in that back door and discover what's inside." Terror gripped me once again. It took several weeks before I could actually imagine, in my mind's eye, opening that door and entering the house. When I did, a flood of memories and experiences were exposed—brought out of darkness and into the light.

So began a twenty-three-year-long stretch of my journey, where I faced the trauma that had occurred in my childhood and into adulthood. I eventually emerged the emotional conqueror, but my journey still did not end there. In time,

Introduction

I would discover that freedom and peace do not come as a one-and-done, but rather as a journey—an expedition—that continually opens up into yet another new territory to be explored.

Thus, just five years ago, I yet again found myself deep in grief, with no awareness of why. Unable to find relief using the therapeutic skills I had learned over the years, I was stumped. As I had been out of therapy for several years, I reached out to a third therapist (now my current therapist) for support and help.

I had no idea that before me lay a whole new dimension of my journey. It was no longer about what had happened to me or what I had overcome—now, the journey was an invitation to discover the impact of what had occurred in my life. I would discover how I viewed myself, how my past still influenced my reactions toward others, and how my fears held me back. There were areas of my life that I had not fully revealed to anyone. Although the fear of rejection and judgment had been diluted, it continued to hover over me.

Whenever my fears rose up, my patient and kind therapist would tell me, "I am here for you, as long as you need me, until you find your peace." Somehow, this became the encouragement I needed to enter this next phase of my expedition.

Eventually, I came to the place where I felt I had found my peace and was thinking that my time with this therapist was nearly complete. "Write your story," he suggested. "You need to find your voice." A new tidal wave of fear crashed over me.

It was this reaction that confirmed to me that he was right. Writing *Treasure Found* has been a huge piece to discovering an increased level of freedom that was awaiting me, as well as uncovering the forthrightness I would need to share this part of my story with you, the reader.

Our stories hold our experiences of life, but we rarely recognize them as stories because the majority slip so quickly from our sight. We barely remember them, unless they have an emotional impact on us: something funny, sad, frightening, out of the ordinary, threatening, or awe inspiring. It is then we will find ourselves sharing the most impactful stories of our day with a family member, friend, coworker—even a stranger or bartender. It often begins with someone asking, "How was your day?" The opening has been offered, and we must decide if it is safe to tell the truth or if we will bypass it with a noncommittal response.

When we hear a person's story, it can stir something within us as we find ourselves relating to what has been shared. Stories connect us (and at times divide us), but they most certainly have the power to awaken what has lain dormant, waiting to surface, thus giving us the opportunity to be curious. This can lead us to a richer understanding of things we never consciously knew about ourselves.

Telling my story in this book has led me to both discover and acknowledge the treasure of who I am. I am a person of courage who has something to offer this life. The attempts of others to destroy me have failed. I not only survived but went on to live a life that has made a difference—both for myself and for others.

Introduction

That first therapist years ago was right: the rotten corpse I had believed was there actually lay over buried treasure.

There is a treasure within you that is waiting for you to find it. You may have doubts that such a treasure even exists. You may have layered it over with false ideas about what defines treasure, or you may have come to believe that your treasure has been permanently stolen, never to be located again. But the greatest adventure you could embark upon begins with finding an infinitesimal amount of hope that the richest of treasures lies within you—just waiting to be found.

1

The Mirror, Part II

The darkened hag speaks to me again in my mind.

"You have exiled me into a tidy box labeled 'Eliminated.' You cannot eliminate me just because you have come to see yourself in a new light. I am the part of you that you must come to understand. I am the layers of beliefs you carried as truths for most of your life!

"Yes, you did process these beliefs, but you never untangled the complexity of how each stained you and how you carry them with you still. You don't have to believe that this is true, but you must come to see that it is true. It is imperative that you see me for who I am and accept the truth that I offer, because I cannot be who you are until you face who I am."

Her words castigate me.

As I listen, I can feel strings of connection begin to form, ever so slowly, between my heart and my mind. None of this is clear to me yet, but I am starting to understand how my past left behind a cloud of debris that still lingers.

A deluge of questions fills my mind.

What part of my past—with all its horrors, suffering, and abuse—have I unknowingly carried with me? Have I come to view the debris of my past as a flaw in my character, believing I must beat this weakness into submission? Have I come to ignore how past indoctrinations affect the way I react to others (even myself)—leaving me feeling regret and guilt? Have I deceived myself by only viewing myself through the lens of all the atrocities I have overcome?

I have to take a break. My head is spinning. I need fresh air and water to center myself.

Eventually, I return to the spot where this encounter with my other self in the mirror began. Taking a deep breath, I close my eyes and re-enter where I left off, fully aware that I cannot steer this course set for me. As difficult as this is, finding the truth is now my objective.

I am at the threshold of seeing that there are two sets of truths and two sets of lies. What might appear to be a lie can, in fact, hold elements of truth. If I overlook this underlying truth, I risk denying or dismissing what I do not yet understand.

My chair is right where I left it. I sit, less reluctantly this time. Across from me sits my darkened self, perhaps now half a shade lighter, less rage on her face. She picks up the mirror, placing it in front of me again. My image reflects back to me, revealing lines of resignation imprinted on my face.

If I have been brought here to face a hidden truth, I think to myself, *it will do me no good to run from it now, because that truth would only run alongside me. There is no escape—I have come too far. I must face this.*

The Mirror, Part II

We sit in silence for some minutes. When I glance her way, I still cannot embrace that this is me, for I have come to know myself only through the lens of having faced the lies in my life with truth. Now, sitting here across from me is a self who appears to be a lie, and yet she holds a truth for me to see and to accept.

How can I ever accept the darkness she has attributed to me? I question. *I've worked so hard to face and heal what I have endured. It took me years to overcome the guilt and shame due to my past. Will I feel all those feelings again if I explore why she has spoken these horrific things to me?*

I realize I do not fear that I will feel shame or guilt, because I now have an awareness of the truth about myself. I have owned my actions—even if they were a result of what others did to me.

Why is she here? I wonder. *What more does she want of me or want to tell me?*

Something she said earlier comes to mind: "It is imperative that you see me and accept the truth that I offer, because I cannot be who you are until you face who I am."

I look up at her and say, "Okay, let's do this. What truth do you offer me?"

She pauses, sits back in her chair, and lowers the mirror in front of me. She begins rubbing her forehead with the index and middle finger of her right hand, in a back-and-forth motion, eyes lowered. She appears to be in a world that I know nothing of. I wait for her words, but she offers none.

I take a deep breath and lean back in my chair.

She abruptly stops, leaning forward to grab my attention with her piercing eyes, and speaks with urgency. "You have not made the connection to what still resides in your mind.

"What lurks in your mind is more than fear. I am what was programmed into you. I am your compulsion. I am your protection, your barrier by using judgment, hate, anger, and fear. I am what you withhold. I am your hiddenness. I am your avoidance. I am your performance. I am your guardedness. I am your secrets. I am all the things you refuse to ask for or to say. I am your doubts. I am your failure. I am your ignorance. I am your shame and humiliation. I am your disgust that you hold toward yourself and toward others. I am your prejudice against the extremist right and left, against legalistic religions, crazy drivers, and those who challenge you. I am your terror of school. Need I go on?"

"No," I answer. Tears brim in my eyes. I want to cry aloud, but dare not. I need to be strong.

I process her list, and in my mind, I add more. *She is my lethargy. She is my excuses. She is my times of lostness. She is the angst. She is what disquiets me. She is my panic and adrenaline rushes. She is my pain and suffering.*

The list could go on, but I get the meaning of this side of me and what she has been carrying for so long. We sit in silence.

I need to speak, but I'm reluctant to feel the compassion that is beginning to rise within me. I've labored so long to eliminate lies from my life. But I now see that what I have discarded became a burden that this darkened hag has carried alone.

I turn toward her. Her face is lighter in color, but her cheeks are still sunken in, her eyes downcast. I know she is exhausted. I approach her slowly and place my right hand cautiously on her shoulder. To my surprise, she allows it to remain there.

My words come out as nearly a whisper. "I see. I see you. I see. I . . . see . . . you."

I continue, unable to stop the tears that begin to fall from my eyes. "I hear you. I really hear you, and I am deeply grieved that I have not been able to understand, let alone receive, the truth that you have carried for so long.

"You're right, I have tried to eliminate you, or at least hide you. I wanted only to heal and rise above the stench of my past, to become the person I believed I could be. But you have paid the price for this, because I did not even know you were there within me. I am truly sorry. I did this because I could not accept that so many people had violated me and weighed me down with how I was to think and to feel. I have been controlled by fear."

She looks up and draws closer to me. Laying her head on my chest, she says, "So long, so long I have carried what you could not. I need your help. Please, I need help."

"Of course, absolutely—you have it."

She appears so weak that I am unsure she will be able to remain standing. As she speaks, her voice is weaker, and I have to lean in to hear her say, "I need rest—a place to rest."

My response is immediate. "Yes! I have a place for you with everything that you need to rest."

I place my arm around her waist and lead her to a room within my home that I have prepared for her. A room within myself. No one has ever been allowed entry before, but as we enter, the fragrance of newness and fresh morning air fills this space, welcoming both of us into its refuge.

The walls are light periwinkle in color; the windows open wide to see the vista of mountains and meadows spread out before us. The king-size bed is made up with a pure white down comforter and several pillows to rest her head upon. In the corner opposite the windows, a wicker rocking chair awaits her, should she choose to use it. From the bathroom adjacent to her bed comes the sound of running water. Her bath is filled to the top, ready for her to slip in and bathe.

Reluctant at first, she eventually decides to step into the warmth of the clear, purifying water. She feels the years of grime melt from her body, and her face reflects a look of peace that softens it.

A pile of large, soft towels awaits. She chooses to put on a summer set of white cotton pajamas. When she emerges, she is not the same self I had been looking at all day. She is still frail and weak, but the darkness has lifted from her face. She is no longer the one I feared—she is instead one who I know needs healing and rest.

I lead her over to the bed, pull back the covers, and help her into crisp, clean, never-before-used sheets. She releases a deep sigh and melts into the mattress. As she places her head on the pillows, she sighs again.

I speak softly to her, "Rest well. I am here with you. I know there is more for me to see and to understand in being fully reconciled with you, but I am not leaving. I will not give up. I accept you as myself."

As I turn to leave her, she speaks in a faint, disappearing voice. "I am grateful . . . for you."

Turning her body onto her left side, she falls into a long-awaited sleep. I trust it will bring her healing, peace, and relief.

I return to my external reality, experiencing the valuable transition that has taken place within me. It is well with my mind and soul.

Reflection on My Story

It was terrifying to face my shadow, that part of me I had kept hidden, hoping others would never discover it. In finding the courage to meet her face-to-face, I discovered newfound freedom, resolution, and, yes, peace.

The day after this encounter with my shadow, she awakened from her deeply exhausted sleep, appearing as me—fully me. Since that day, I have not doubted my authentic identity. As I move through life, I continue to discover and evolve into the person I was created to be. I find that I am rarely in conflict with myself, but when I am, I am less apt to delay facing and owning what is going on within me, instead truly listening to the needs I have been ignoring.

In no way am I now perfect—far from it—but I can see my imperfections as an opportunity to process and change. I see them as hindrances that are holding me back from the truth about myself.

I do not deny that this discovery was a mammoth challenge. I had to choose to deal with it, dismiss it as unimportant, ignore it, or even justify my shadow's existence. This took courage—a heck of a lot of courage—but the end result was worth it.

Two of Carl Jung's quotes nicely sum up this tension for me:

"Shadow work is the path of the heart warrior."

"Knowing your shadow self is vital if you wish to bring harmony into your life."

On that day of reckoning, my breakthrough resulted not only from facing my shadow self but also from being able to incorporate the culmination of the months and years of facing the roadblocks that had been positioned in my life. My victory did not happen with a quick-fix answer but rather by taking one step at a time, accepting each challenge that appeared before me.

The Mirror, Part II

What Is Your Story?

As I stated at the beginning, no two experiences are the same. I have heard of many who have had a gentle and loving exchange with their shadow self, while others have had a great debate with theirs, like I did. The shadow is often the very part of yourself that you have rejected. Whatever your situation, I assure you that choosing to accept what you formerly believed should be rejected will offer you newfound freedom.

Have you experienced the voice of the shadow within you?

What message of truth did it want to convey to you?

What was your response? Fear? A desire to ignore it? Did you try to explain it away or to label it as an annoyance, sin, or something else?

As Carl Jung said, "Until you make the unconscious conscious, it will direct your life, and you will call it fate."

Share Your Story

In facing your shadow self, I encourage you to share your story. That said, I would also encourage you to do this with a professional therapist if you have faced trauma, abuse, or neglect in your life. This also holds true if you deal with depression, an anxiety disorder, or other emotional or mental health issues. Your care and well-being are of utmost importance. There are well-trained professionals who will walk you through what may feel threatening in listening to what your shadow self wants to reveal to you.

If you struggle with how to start, you might begin with sharing secrets that you have never shared (see chapter 3). There is a beginning to each journey of discovery, and this may be a way for you to embark on yours.

Another entry point may be that you test the waters with someone you trust to see if they are open to hearing about some of the difficult situations you may have faced in life. There is no set guidebook. Listen to your feelings and use wisdom to discern with whom you should share your experiences. When you risk with the right person, you will open up the flow of what you have knowingly or unknowingly built a dam around.

2

What Might Have Been

Mrs. Donnelly terrified me. She was my civics teacher during my senior year of high school. I remember her as not an attractive woman. Cropped red hair, short in stature, with a pointy nose, she wanted to be popular and made a vigorous effort to charm the brightest and most popular students.

During the first few weeks I was in her class, I began to hate her. I mean *hate* her! Her pandering to the popular students—and those same students sucking up to her in return—disgusted me. The brightest students always evoked within me strong feelings of intimidation and powerlessness. In turn, whenever I saw Mrs. Donnelly stroking the egos of her future academic stars, it enraged me because I didn't fit into that group. I would focus my rage onto her, angered that her attention to her star students made me feel invisible.

I honestly had no idea where this hatred came from, but it was a deep reservoir within that held a potential eruption of emotion. Outwardly, I was kind, respectful, quiet, and generous. I withheld every dark thought that came across my mind. I could not accept that I had such dark and ominous thoughts inside me.

But more and more venomous images continued to form in my mind with every passing day I sat in her class.

As the ominous holiday of Halloween approached, I began to imagine ways of destroying Mrs. Donnelly. I noted that students often left her gifts on her desk: flowers, candy, candles.

Seeing how others showered her with gifts, I laid out my own diabolical plan. I would find a way to inject a caramel apple with poison. I would sneak into her classroom before morning classes and leave it on her desk.

For four weeks, I played out this fantasy in my mind, calculating what I would do to avoid getting caught. I had to find a poison I could put into the apple that she would not taste. This dark plan became my obsession every day that I sat in class. Part of me feared I might follow through with it.

I despised her giggles and the way she joked with her select group, because I was ignored. Yet I wanted to be ignored, because if she called upon me, it would mean humiliation. Teachers calling on me almost always ended in humiliation, and there was no way in hell I was going to be her next victim.

If anyone was going to be a victim . . . it was going to be her!

Years later, in my midthirties, I was unprepared for a sudden tidal wave of grief that crashed over me—a wave whose origin was a mystery. I had been basking in the emotional sunlight of joy and freedom for five years now—a reward achieved from dealing with issues that had come up for me as a parent and wife. I would eventually come to call these years my "becoming a better person by doing 'feel-good' therapy" season.

Yet what I was now experiencing was something far more threatening—an inner turmoil I never could have imagined, even back in those days in Mrs. Donnelly's class. I felt wave after wave of sadness, uncertainty, and fear, along with a growing restlessness that I found impossible to quiet or redirect.

It had never crossed my mind that there could be something left to face from my past. I falsely believed that if I had resolved something, that meant I was done with it. My life would be fixed, and I would arrive at a peaceful existence that would last for the rest of my life. Yet emerging before me, I saw questions I needed to navigate. It was a process that would lead into unexplored caverns deep beneath the surface of my consciousness.

Regret was something I had, until now, refused to get sucked into. My thinking was, *Why have regrets when we must face each day and deal with whatever life throws our way?* I had observed far too many people carrying a list of regrets that left them stagnant, stuck, and, for some, even immobilized. For me, this was too high a price to pay. Life is meant to be lived, and we are meant to deal with the bumps and disappointments that come along with it.

But when my tidal wave of grief came after me, it was not regret that it carried—it was pain, terror, hopelessness, and with it all, the barrage of questions that had first begun to emerge when I was a teenager. Now, with adulthood, these questions were more refined, bringing the realization that I had more to explore.

Why was I born into the particular family that was mine to call home? Why hadn't I been protected?

Why wasn't I taught how to learn, and why had I not been mentored in my learning with encouragement and support? What would have happened if a teacher had helped me along the way, instead of allowing me to slip through the cracks? What if I had not been terrified of school and had loved learning because I felt safe? Could I really have been whatever I wanted to be? Where would life have taken me? Would I have met my lifelong partner/husband at college or in graduate school? Would I have had the perfect wedding I dreamed of as a child? Would I have never faced the pain of divorce?

How would I be helping the world if I could have had a career—one that I first imagined stepping into and then achieved as a goal? Would the damaging choices I made never have occurred, because I had confidence in myself and felt grounded in my true identity? Would I have bypassed more than thirty years of believing I was ignorant and stupid?

What would have happened if the people who had access to me had not abused me?

The questions kept coming, and with each question, I felt the rise of more grief, loss, and an anger that came with internalized screams of *What if . . . ?* And *Why?*

When I finally came up for air, I knew I needed a plan. Would I dismiss these questions? *Oh well, it is what it is.* Would I override my feelings? *Faith, get over it and move on. Life is life and everyone suffers!* Or would I honor each rising question with respect, for the purpose of realizing all I had lost and missed out on? Would I have the courage to face the origins of my life coming unraveled?

If I chose to face the unanswered questions that rose into my consciousness, it would require me to face each experience and emotion with honesty, not dismissing what the answers would reveal. Denial and avoidance would need to be short-lived and overridden, should I decide to step into the assignment that my inner wisdom was offering to me.

So many years have passed since being in Mrs. Donnelly's class. That storm of questions that arose within me as a teenager set me on quest for answers. In time, I did face the truth of what had happened to me. Eventually, I began to align this truth alongside my experiences of joy, happiness, and beauty—experiences that were also a part of my life. These opposing realities left me to wrestle with the tension of living in the truth of both/and, rather than either/or.

Even among the ashes of what had been taken from me (due to the layers of trauma I experienced), I would find courage and a burning desire not to settle for less than the life of inner peace I believed I could experience. I became a seeker to find the answer—to find an escape from what plagued me.

I did not have any psychological knowledge at the beginning of my journey, so I could not see how the circumstances of my life had influenced my behaviors and decisions—decisions that impacted me both in negative and positive ways. What I did have was an inner compass of wisdom that continually guided me to stay on course to find answers and change my life. One thought kept me steadfast in my search: *This is not it. There must be more for me than this—something better for my life.*

I debated whether to give you, the reader, the ending of my story here at the beginning of this book. I concluded that I wanted you to know this: all the tears that I shed, the terror within memories I endured, the courage it took for me not to quit—all of it was worth it. I had to heal from the the experiences I faced as a child and as a young adult in order to be freed of their lasting impact. Each step taken through these dark nights of my soul was worth the freedom I obtained in the end.

So, where am I today? Here is a slice of my current story at the time of this writing.

It is late November, and I am sitting at a table overlooking the city. A white cloth covers the table, an elegant place setting upon it. This is one of my husband David's and my favorite restaurants. Today is not only Thanksgiving; it is also our thirty-eighth anniversary. I am married to the love of my life who sits across from me, and I am filled with gratitude thinking of all the ways David has been there for me over the years. He has loved me well with his care, support, and insight into my life. He has allowed me to be truly myself as I navigated the passageways that led to my freedom.

As we reflect on our life together, we are content with what we have created. We recognize that the early years of struggle in our relationship were difficult but also worth it. Each stressful phase we walked through revealed areas within each of us that needed to be faced. In turn, our challenges directed us to evolve as individuals. Loving each other well meant we would support what was needed for our emotional, intellectual, and personal development, showing compassion and patience toward each other in the process.

Did we always do this perfectly? Of course not. We both had unresolved pain that would flare up inside us. But because we were faithful to each other and ourselves to become whole as human beings, we faced it head-on. And that journey continues.

Between us, we have five daughters, eleven grandchildren, and four sons-in-law. Each has left their mark on our lives with their incredible uniqueness. Each in their own way has encouraged us to see our areas of limitation as parents and grandparents. We have not always perfectly understood them or consistently responded with wise and heartfelt compassion. They have been our teachers as much as we have tried to be theirs, and we count it all joy and a blessing to have them in our lives.

As I look back over the years, I can see that through the difficulty and time spent healing my life—amid the swamp-filled yuck I had to walk through—I also *lived* my life. I gave birth to three daughters, was an entrepreneur, created numerous businesses, and established two nonprofits (one for adult survivors of childhood abuse). I used my creative giftedness and love for teaching to share my story in a way that made a difference throughout the city and beyond.

I have walked through many seasons and have come to realize that because I am a visionary, my life was not meant to land in one place. I always see new possibilities at each intersection.

At the age of eighteen, I had my one and only employed position, for three weeks. It was for Montgomery Ward in their catalog department. Over the Christmas season, I did such a fantastic job as a temporary employee that they wanted to hire me full-time. Three weeks working in that company made me realize I could not work for anyone. My hidden entrepreneur had awakened, and the journey to something more soon emerged.

In my first marriage, at the age of nineteen, I learned how to be a businessperson. I faced my fears of failure or feeling stupid and expressed my visionary self by creating several businesses. The Burlap Bag sold records and mod (i.e., hippie-era) gifts, Dock 22 was an import shop, and Good Times Ice Cream Parlor & Restaurant was literally built from the ground up—building and all—and featured singing servers. The Tourist Shop off I-90 in South Dakota offered strange touristy items and exclusive gifts to vacationers headed west. The Carousel was a gift store that not only sold exclusive gifts but also pianos, organs, and record LPs. But it was my longstanding fireworks business, which imported, wholesaled, and retailed colorful wonders to light up the night sky, that allowed for the full force of my creative business skills to come to life.

After divorcing, I continued in the fireworks business on my own. At the same time, I developed other interests, in addition to being involved in the lives of my family.

I loved singing and sang in auditioned groups, a choir, and even had a part in a musical at a megachurch I attended. I had never acted before, but when chosen for the part, I jumped into it. I must admit, it was fun and terrifying all at the same time to act and sing on stage. Even though I was told I was quite successful, the terror of forgetting my lines was too much for me. Once was enough, and I knew that acting in *any* form was not for me—but I had tried it.

Around the age of forty, I battled to keep my business when the Secretary of State took on the fireworks industry, and I lost. After twenty-one years in the business, my life abruptly changed. Liquidating as quickly as possible, I avoided both business and personal bankruptcy. It soon became clear, however, that this change would mean downsizing everything that I had worked so hard to obtain. I walked away from a business that had been with me for half of my life. I sold our luxury home and nice cars, moving into a much smaller house in a town outside the city.

This intersection was terribly painful for me. I was forced to see how much of my identity I had put into being competent and successful. I had begun to see my trophies as my identity. It took me two years to process out my anger and resentment over losing what I had thought defined me as an overcomer—and how that had somehow made me a "legitimate" human being.

After my two-year tantrum, the next nine years were a threshold of change in my life. I had originally resented the place I had landed to live, but in time it became a refuge where I would face my inner self. I would come to see that I was more than my success. I found my value and my truth, and I came to experience the Divine in a whole new light. My eyes were opened to a deeper meaning, and I began to see myself through a lens offered from a Being far greater than myself. And no, I was not high on drugs.

These discoveries came from long and honest walks where I cried, got angry, screamed, and opened myself up to a deeper truth for my existence. The many unanswered questions I had in high school began to be answered, one by one. I began to settle, and peace became a developing friendship.

When I moved away from the place that I had for eleven years called "my desert," I wept. Even though I was moving to a lovely home in a location I had always dreamed of, I was leaving what had become my sanctuary—the place where I had awakened to begin to fully experience life. Over those eleven years that I lived on the outskirts of that city, I healed many of the deep wounds of my heart. I realized that I had been given the gift of seeing my *being* as good.

It has been twenty years now since that move. I continue to learn the art of living in my true self and sustaining that life. I am alert to the lies that may still rise in my mind out of nowhere, and have gotten surprisingly good at sorting out truth from fiction. This has been necessary for me to maintain the centering pulse of my peace, truth, and goodness.

So, whatever happened to Mrs. Donnelly? Obviously, she did not meet her demise. Halloween came and went that year, and I never acted on my impulse to harm her. I didn't even give her a healthy apple. My hate for her was real, but I was never able to cause her harm, nor was I motivated to do so. Here is what finally happened.

I struggled in her class and found myself barely passing that first semester. I hid in the back row, never raising my hand to answer any question proposed to the class. By the second semester, I was less than passing, and as the end of the year neared, my weekly grades assured me that I was not likely to pass her class. This would mean I would not graduate. As the weeks ticked by, I began to panic, knowing that the civics final was coming in a couple of weeks.

Mrs. Donnelly let us know that the final exam would consist of authoring an essay, choosing from one of three questions. Not knowing what those questions would be, I felt that studying would be a waste at this point.

The day of the final arrived, and I walked into class, hoping that I would be able to write something—anything. My palms were sweaty, my heart was beating quickly, and I found myself shutting out everything around me as adrenaline released throughout my body. The sheet of questions was passed out, and the timer was set for one hour. "Class, begin," Mrs. Donnelly announced.

When I looked at the list of three questions, one stood out to me. It was about the Vietnam War, and the question was, "Define the DMZ zone, the conflict in that area, the political differences, and possible resolutions."

In an instant, I imagined a living story and began to author my essay in story form. With each sentence, I found myself in the experience of a farmer on one side of the DMZ and another farmer on the other side. I was a bit astounded that this information had lodged somewhere in my mind yet that I had not known it was there. I had been in my seat each day throughout the year. Somehow I had absorbed the information Mrs. Donnelly taught me, enabling me to write my story.

I completed my essay ahead of time and had just begun rereading it when the timer's ding went off, sounding the end of the hour. I walked to the front of the classroom, handed in my paper, and left—not knowing if this would lead to a passing grade that might allow me to graduate or to the need for me to repeat this class.

The following week was graduation. Everyone in our senior class had to walk the stage in cap and gown, not knowing if we had passed or failed. It was school policy. They handed out an empty engraved-leather diploma holder to each student. The actual diploma would be given out the following week, and some students—like myself—were left to worry if we would graduate.

My name was called, and I walked across the stage to collect my empty folder. I shook the right hands of the principal and of someone else standing there, likely the school superintendent. I then walked off the stage, down the steps, and exited behind the curtain. As I descended the stairs, I saw a group of teachers standing behind stage directing students back to the auditorium. Several offered congratulations to students as they passed by.

I saw at once that Mrs. Donnelly was among the teachers standing there. Her eyes locked with mine, and she moved toward me. My heart rate increased, and I dropped my eyes, hoping I could pass her as quickly as possible—but that was not going to happen.

As we moved toward each other, she said, "Faith, I want to speak to you." My heart sank. *Crap, here it comes*, I thought. *I failed and she is letting me know this now.*

As I stepped out of the line, she looked at me with a serious but nonthreatening look. She continued, "Faith, I want to apologize to you. I did not acknowledge you as a student who had potential. I misjudged and ignored you.

Your essay was astounding, amazing, and creative. I gave you an A-plus. You passed my class. You graduated. I am sorry that I did not see you."

I was in shock, and I do not remember what I said or did next. I was filled with immediate relief and excitement yet also stunned by her apology.

Over the years, I have imagined that I made an impact on how she saw all her students from that day forward. At least I hope so.

That year in her class, all my darkness had been repressed back into my inner abyss. I was too young to understand or to connect my reactions to the hate that lay within, or to the darker meaning Halloween held for me.

Reflection on My Story

The terror of school I carried from fourth grade into high school was real. I attended school faithfully because I had to, but I dreaded every day that I went. For me, learning was never about discovery but about carrying the fear of being humiliated and failing. It was about survival. I hid in the classes that I dreaded the most and went forward in the classes where I felt safe or excelled. Each day, I was either withdrawing or emerging. Most often I did both, several times in a day. But I survived.

I have cried and grieved as I've felt the pain of all that I lost due to not being able to enjoy what my school experience could have been for me. *What could I have become if only my parents and teachers had been able to recognize just how lost I was—surviving each day immersed in fear?*

I carried this fear of education—of tests, of being taught, critiqued, or challenged—for much of my life. I realized that this deeply lodged fear had not only penetrated how I had come to see myself but also had an impact on how I'd learned to cope every day as a survivor. Knowing this, I was able to begin to grieve what I had lost.

It was then that I was able to accept what could have been. This made it possible to accept all that I *had* overcome.

The chapters in front of you are stories from my past. Each one holds pieces of the puzzle that became a part of the journey that guided me into the hardest work I have ever done. But as I have stated numerous times throughout the years, if I had to do it all over again to be where I am today, I would do it—because being where I am today is more than good. I am free, no longer just surviving life—I am now *living* life.

What's Your Story?

When have you not felt seen and valued?
How did this make you feel?
How did you resolve this experience in your life?

SHARE YOUR STORY

Have you ever shared your personal experience? In sharing your story, you will uncover how the story has inserted itself into your life.

It's never too late to share your most recent or earliest experiences with someone.

3

Secrets

I leave Rich's office, methodically moving toward the staircase running up from the garden level to the first floor. With each step, a numbing heaviness compresses my legs. My chest tightens; my breathing becomes increasingly shallow. My right hand grips the wooden railing that is currently the only tangible connection I have to reality.

Whatever struck a chord within me during the therapy session is unclear, but an emotional storm is brewing. I'm agitated and uncomfortable. *What is it?* I wonder to myself.

I head for the exit, reassuring myself that I am okay; I just need to get outside so I can breathe. Pushing the door open, I smell the fragrant mountain air. I pause to lift my head toward the sky, allowing the spring current to flow over my face. I inhale.

For a few brief moments, I believe I have made it to safety, away from the inner onslaught of emotions I am experiencing. I focus on my car in the parking lot. It becomes my goal, but I am unable to silence the message that is increasing in urgency, on a loop within my mind: *It is time. No more secrets.*

Panic rushes over me as I walk the short distance to my car. This eruption of terror carries with it a lava flow of messages that I do not want to hear.

What about the rage you feel toward truck drivers who are aggressive toward you on the road? What about the times you feel a reactionary contempt toward a person who falsely accuses, judges, or challenges you? You never told anyone about the times your first husband manipulated you into doing things you never would have imagined doing. And remember when you betrayed your friend? Don't forget that experience you swore you would never speak of, and the half-truths you've told to avoid shame, and . . .

With each ominous question that presents something I never speak of, my reality darkens.

I reach my car, unlocking it quickly. I jump inside just as I erupt into tears. "I can't! I just cannot do this," I scream. A blanket of overwhelming inevitability seems to tighten around me.

Through my sobs, I whisper over and over again, "I really can't do this; I just cannot do this."

Inner excitement grew as my husband, David, and I approached the large local church hosting an evening with Paul Young, author of *The Shack*. His book had spread like wildfire throughout the country. There was something about this author that made me sense I had to see him for myself.

I had first heard of Paul Young's book from a friend who was deeply affected by the story.

"It's an absolute must-read," he had told me, sharing where I could order it. When it arrived, I started reading, and I did not put the book down until I had finished.

Paul's story affected me for many reasons. I related to how his main character intentionally stepped into the pain of his past to seek healing and found compassion and understanding offered to him. I, too, had faced my own painful past over the years and had been offered supportive care and wisdom on my journey.

I sensed this author had suffered in ways that were similar to how I had suffered. That evening, Paul shared more of his own personal story, describing his loss and trauma, while adding the insights and freedom that facing his past had brought him.

Paul was vulnerable in sharing his personal story—his backstory to writing *The Shack*. As he unfolded each layer of his past, it became clear that we did indeed have a great deal in common. His early childhood was all too familiar to me—different circumstances but similar outcomes.

His dad was a minister and a missionary, which aligned closely with my dad being a minister. At one point I thought, *I think we grew up in the same denomination.* Thirteen years later, I heard Paul name the denomination his dad had been affiliated with, and I was right!

My heart broke for both our pasts that night. How prevalent child abuse is. Even in places where you expect a child to be cared for and protected, there often lurks a predator, lying in wait.

What I was unprepared for that evening was a sentence Paul would share that would lodge deep into my subconscious to germinate. It would take six years for it to sprout. Six years for me to fully experience the truth that he spoke that evening.

"I have no more secrets."

Spoken with complete honesty, freedom, and sincerity, this heart-gripping sentence was an emotional lightning bolt, hitting somewhere between my heart and belly.

How is it even possible not to have any secrets? I thought.

Paul went on, "I have no secrets that my wife, my kids, and my friends do not know."

I could not even imagine what he was saying. I had been taught to not share everything, because it could be destructive or hurtful or cause others unnecessary pain. I had openly shared my life, my past, and my abuse with my therapist. I had shared those therapy sessions with my husband and closest friends, concluding that I was being real—fully vulnerable and honest. All this was based on what I believed to be honest truth. I had even publicly shared stories of my past.

But as Paul's statement caused me to pause, a clear memory of my mother's long-held secret came into focus. She had leaked bits and pieces of it over the years, but she had never fully disclosed the details.

I'm seventeen, sitting at the breakfast table filling out applications for college, when I come across a question to which I have no answer to place on the blank line before me. Only my dad is present.

"Dad, is Mom's maiden name Williams, Roseland, or Parsons?"

My grandmother's last name, Williams, has never made much sense to me. I have long been confused about our family tree. Over the years I have heard various last names floating around. I don't have much interest in genealogy, but now, however, I need an answer to the question: Mother's Maiden Name.

My dad pauses. His pause becomes an extended silence.

I look up at him, awaiting his answer.

Finally, he takes a deep breath, "None of those are your mother's maiden name. Her maiden name is Dischinger."

"What? Seriously?" I'm in shock. "How did I not know this? Why was I never told? Who is Dischinger?"

Dad goes on to tell me that my mother's father was a disgrace to her and that she had no respect for him. He was never at home, only in and out at times to see my mother and her two siblings, leaving soon after. Shame held my mother victim to a secret she kept hidden. She hates her maiden name, holds her alcoholic father in disgust, and has chosen never to speak of him.

Eventually, I would come to see how my mother's secret had wrapped itself around her. It held her hostage to shame, causing her to view herself in a negative light.

Over the next few years, Paul's statement about having no secrets would periodically float into my consciousness. I would continue to debate internally whether anyone was capable of not having any secrets.

Did I feel like there were things I had never told anyone? Not really. But then, just when I would come to this conclusion, a thought would bubble up, carrying with it a message: *What about this or what about that?* I could easily put my answer to these questions into the category that this was something that might hurt someone. Because of this fact, it was obviously not a secret to be told.

Some years after hearing Paul Young speak, I again learned that he was holding a conference in North Carolina for the weekend. My husband and I thought it might be a good idea to attend. Plus, we had never been to North Carolina and a mini-vacation seemed nice.

I observed Paul many times over that weekend, always acting consistently with who he'd said he was when I first heard him speak. He had no secrets; he lived from his authentic self, and if anything, his insights and wisdom had increased with time.

That weekend, Paul once again repeated, "I have no more secrets."

There it was again, that hit to the chest. This time, it carried with it the rest of the memory of my mother's long-held secret.

Secrets

I recalled the torment my mother went through in withholding her deepest secret. As she entered her dying days, she became more agitated and reactive. I told her one afternoon, "Mom, you are tormented. You need to speak with someone."

"Yes, I am a tormented woman!" she lambasted me. "I will never speak of things that only my husband knows."

I offered again, "Mom, you need to share at least some of what you are feeling with a person you can trust. Do you want me to call your minister?"

She nodded okay. Her pastor showed up later that same day, and they spoke together in private. Mom later told me how comforting it was to have someone be kind to her and share comforting words from Scripture. But she did not share her torment with him.

Family gathered to be with her over the next days. She continued to fade, but at times she would lash out at me over things of little consequence or make caustic statements that would cut deep into my heart.

On the night before her passing, our family took a break for dinner. I was asked to come back to sign papers for hospice to take over her case. The nurse told me that they were now giving her morphine. By the time I returned, my mother would be out—asleep—under the power of pain medication.

After dinner, I told my family to go home and rest. I would sign the necessary papers and be home shortly. It was late, and I was exhausted from the up-and-down vigil I had been keeping with my mother for months.

But when I arrived back at my mother's bedside, I did not find her knocked out from the medication. Instead, she was rocking back and forth, agitated, moaning, and panicky. She was reacting to something she was obviously experiencing.

I approached and sat on the bed next to her. "Mom, it's okay. I'm here."

Her hand swiped at me to push me away.

"Mom, what is it? What is bothering you?"

As soon as I asked the question, an inner knowing rose within me. *Don't call her Mom. Call her Ellie. Speak to her by her childhood nickname.*

"Ellie? Ellie, it's okay. I'm here. What is happening? What are you afraid of?"

Her response was distraught and panicked. "Get him off of me! Get him *off* me!"

I softly spoke to her, "Get who off you? Who is it?"

"Billy! Get him off me."

It was then I had the validation of what I had long suspected. Her dad's name was William Dischinger—"Billy" was his nickname. Mom had once told me that, when she was twelve, her dad had come by and taken her and her mother for a chocolate soda at a local drug store. As they left, my mother promptly threw up the soda at the curb. Her comment to me was that she always felt sick around him. That day she threw up the treat she loved most—chocolate sodas.

I continued, "Ellie, what did Billy do?"

"He is on top of me. Get him off me. He's hurting me."

It was difficult for her to get focused enough to offer exact details. The large dose of morphine was causing her confusion.

I recalled other information from the past that she had offered. Her dad had been killed by a train on the tracks. It was thought that he was drunk and had fallen asleep there. The horrifying result was that he was decapitated, with other limbs severed as well. His left arm was found, her name tattooed on it: "Ellie." When she learned this, she hated that he had done this, tattooed only *her* name onto his arm.

Why would he have done this when he had other children, as well as a wife, and their names were not found on his body? Why did it appear that he'd given my mother special attention? These were just a few of my many questions that had been left unanswered.

As the after-midnight hours passed, my mother shared more of how Billy was "on her."

Now, not as her daughter but as a counselor, I walked Ellie through the traumatic memory that she had repressed her entire life. The memory of being physically abused and, by her description, an act of sexual abuse that she had vowed never to tell anyone but her husband. This was the memory that had left her tormented.

I helped her to get rid of Billy, assuring her repeatedly that what he did was not her fault—it was his. She was innocent, and what he did to her should never have happened.

Around two a.m., she finally took a deep breath, relaxed, and soon fell asleep. In the late afternoon of that day, she left this life, leaving behind her secret as well.

As I sit here in my car outside Rich's office, sobbing and screaming that I cannot do this, I know I must quiet my panic. Fortunately, I have the tools to do so. I tell myself to breathe slowly.

Slow, deep breaths. In through the nose—out through the mouth.

I feel a threatening inner stirring—an angst that there is something more than grief I am facing.

For God's sake, why do I have to expose more? There is nothing. What the hell is this feeling? No way is there something more for me to face! Yet why do I feel this impending doom rising within me?

My internal protest does nothing to minimize my argument. If anything, it only increases a barrage of details that, throughout the years, I had believed were insignificant. But these details were now morphing into a whole range of Mount Everests, rising up in front of me to conquer. I was terrified.

It has already been six years since I'd attended that conference in North Carolina with Paul Young. I have been facing a new grief issue that I was unable to fully process on my own. After wrestling with it for a few months, I finally decided I needed to call a professional to help me.

On my first visit, I felt relief walking into Rich's office. It felt safe, and I believed my time with this therapist would be a few brief months, at most. I made it known that he would find no one who would work harder than I.

It seemed incomprehensible that there would be anything unresolved other than this new issue of grief. Whether it had been with friends, family, a therapist, or a stranger, I had shared every dark incident that had ever happened to me. I had also shared, with brokenness, my heartache of how I had impacted others because of my unresolved pain. I was vulnerable. I had exposed myself, revealing all the ugliness of how others had controlled me and the ugliness that I had inflicted onto others.

As I continued to sit in my car for I don't know how long, I became still enough to hear a different internalized message. It was a peaceful voice, separate from the confronting questions that had thrown me into this emotional tailspin.

Faith, yes, you can do this. What you believe are minuscule details from your past that can be ignored or explained away are what is keeping you from stepping into the next phase of your development. It is time. You will do this one step at a time, as you are ready to face what you fear—rejection.

But what if my secrets become my identity? I respond. *What if others see me through the lens of my secrets?*

Over time, however, I discovered that indeed a huge layer of my pain and trauma had been removed years ago during the first phase of my healing journey. I had learned that my identity was *not* my past. That part of my life had healed.

But what was *not* completely resolved was the fallout from my abuse that still lingered. The ashes of my past still held the power to shut me down or cause me to disengage, to overreact to drivers on the road, or to become outraged at others who appeared blind to what was going on around them.

I had made the false assumption that leaving out details from my past was in the best interest of others as well as myself. I had repressed my negative feelings because I believed it was the "right" thing to do. But this only caused them to erupt when I least expected it.

As promised, I worked hard on myself. I spent hours journaling, processing, digging, and discovering. I discovered pieces that still had to be gathered, compiled, and added to the million-piece puzzle of my life. Once I knew he would not turn away, I began to share details more openly with Rich. It wasn't easy to do, but over time I spoke of things that I had minimized and ignored. I even shared things I had never shared with anyone before.

Yes, I am now experiencing more freedom in my life. Can I say with complete confidence, as Paul Young does, "I have no more secrets?" I believe I can say this now, but if there is a nudge from within saying, *What about . . . ,* I have the confidence now to face it, deal with it, and liberate myself.

Reflection on My Story

Whether my secrets were inconsequential or significant, the impact remained the same. Each created a barrier that unknowingly restrained me from living the life I was meant to live, without reservations.

My secrets held the power to shackle my mind and heart in ways I could not see. Once I did—once the spotlight of truth exposed them—I was forced to decide. Would I deal with them or keep them hidden? Would I allow my fear of rejection, judgment, and possible ridicule to tether me to what others might do or think of me? Or would I find the courage to slash the tie that kept me from soaring into the freedom I was meant to experience?

Time and aging did not resolve the secrets in my mother's life. Speaking the truth was what set her free. Sharing my secrets set me free as well, and I am grateful.

What Is Your Story?

Do you have secrets that you have never shared with anyone?

What do you believe would happen if someone knew your secrets?

What influence have secrets had on how you view yourself and live your life?

Share Your Story

To share your secrets with someone may very well be the biggest risk you have ever faced. It takes time to feel safe enough to expose what you have told yourself you would never reveal to anyone. Take the time you need to find the person you can trust. Someone who will hold your sharing in strictest confidence, who will respect you without judgment, and who will honor the courage it took for you to share your secrets.

Sharing your story is worth the courage it will take to honor yourself by speaking the truth. As you drop the weight of your secrets, it will be replaced with liberation. There is nothing that compares to the feeling of being liberated.

4

The Destroyer, Part I: What Happened?

What depraved thoughts ruminated in Ted's mind the day he first saw me? Was he aroused with excitement, with lustful desire in discovering his next victim? Was it the innocence and shyness of a two-year-old that locked his gaze onto me? Did he begin imagining how he would find his way into my parents' lives to gain access to me—cunningly scheming, imagining the day he would have me alone, all to himself? Ted sat quietly that day in the home of one of the church parishioners, hiding his thoughts behind his socially acceptable persona. But his perverse thoughts would all too soon become my reality.

―――

A welcoming reception had been planned for our family, on August 22—a pleasantly warm summer day in Minnesota, as it turned out. My dad had just been called to his second pastorate, and on this day my parents, brothers, and I entered a room filled with strangers who had come to meet us—and to evaluate this new family entering their community.

Many residents in this small town were blond-haired and blue-eyed Swedes and Norwegians, to whom we must have looked quite different. My father, brothers, and I all had dark hair and brown eyes, except for my eldest brother, whose eyes were hazel. Mom had red hair, and both my parents had Brooklyn accents. We must have surely piqued their curiosity with our blend of undefined ethnicity.

My mom had a family tradition: when a guest came into our home, they were asked to sign our guest book. It recorded their names, the date, and a space for a brief comment. On this momentous day, Mom of course had the book with her for all to sign—a lasting memory of that day, and a way for her to place names with faces. Ted's name was there, dated August 22, next to his signature . . . *Ted Larkin*.

To most, Ted was a hardworking farmer, living with his wife and family. His unassuming character disguised him as he went about his daily farming routine. He kept mostly to himself, but there was another side to him—a well-concealed and unsuspected dark side.

My exact age the first time Ted had me alone is not clearly defined. What I do know is that my earliest experience with him was sometime before the age of five.

By the time I reached five years old, my parents wanted me to take piano lessons. They had little money to spare, but they would find a way to make this happen. What they did *not* have money for was a piano. Ted heard about this

The Destroyer, Part I: What Happened?

and told my parents that he would loan us his piano. What he did not tell them was that he planned to make occasional brief visits to hear me play.

One of the first times he "dropped by," Mom and I had been cleaning the parsonage, our Saturday's required task. The doorbell rang, Mom answered it, and there stood Ted. Cold terror ran through me. I grabbed my mother's skirt and cried, "Mommy, don't let him in!"

Ted stood in the doorway looking down at me. His smile was sinister, not friendly. An alarm went off in me, pulsating and surging throughout my body. I *knew* he was a danger.

Again, I pleaded, "Mommy, don't let him in!"

My mom grabbed my arm and pulled me around to stand beside her. She firmly and emphatically said, "Faith, you stop this right now! Mr. Larkin is the good man who is loaning us his piano so you can learn to play. You be nice to him!"

I quickly fell in line. I was an obedient, quiet child. Ted came in and asked me to play something for him. I climbed up on the piano bench and did as I was told. I pressed the keys and played a simple tune—"Hot Cross Buns"—that I had learned from memory.

Ted's rare surprise drop-ins left me never knowing when he might be in my house. I lived in fear of him coming into our space. He would stare at me with his penetrating eyes, never looking away. I would drop my eyes to the floor. My mother's continual warnings not to kick the piano board with my feet or I would scratch his piano only served to increase my fear of this man.

My parents attended prayer conferences and denominational conferences, which meant my brothers and I were placed with different families in the church who were eager to have us join them. Sometimes it would be just for a weekend, but there were other times when, for a week or longer, a conference would take Dad and Mom out of state.

There were wonderful families that I looked forward to being with. But other families not only *felt* unsafe; they *were* unsafe. One such family was related to Ted's, and when this family offered to have me stay with them, we would visit Ted's house.

On one occasion when I was four or five years old, my caretakers drove to Ted's house, and I was of course brought along. There was a room upstairs in Ted's house where I could go and play. There were few toys in this barren room. I remember hearing the adults talking downstairs, as their voices carried into the room above where I sat, all alone.

On this visit, Ted entered the room. Closing the door behind him, he asked if I remembered what he had taught me. I nodded yes, too afraid to speak.

The floor had been painted gray. A braided throw rug lay beside a bed; a small window at the far end of the room allowed some muted light to enter. Except for some shelving with a few books and old toys, the room was mostly empty.

Ted found a white piece of chalk from somewhere in the room and proceeded to draw a circle on the floor. In

The Destroyer, Part I: What Happened?

earlier times when he found ways to have access to me, he had taught me what I was to do when this circle was drawn.

When the two ends of his drawing touched, the circle was complete. I obediently stepped inside the ring separating me from the safety I felt on the opposite side of the thin white line. In total silence, I did what Ted had trained me to do. I removed my clothes and stood in the center of ·the circle, silent.

I froze under Ted's predaceous gaze. I avoided his stare by dropping my eyes to the floor. I succumbed to the powerlessness I felt as Ted's thievery took from me what was not his to have.

I cannot say when Ted first began molesting me and training me to engage in things no child should ever know about. What I do remember is that he terrorized me with his very presence. When he found my weakness—my intense fear of physical pain—a simple excruciating pinch on my skin or a squeeze on the sensitive spot on my shoulder would instantly cause me to fall into silent submission.

My earliest memory with Ted is of a heinous and petrifying experience. I can only assume I was somewhere between the ages of three and four. It was a diabolical night when I was taken to an empty silo.

There were other men in the silo with Ted. I was put into a harness with a rope attached to it. My small body was pulled high above their heads. I was gripped with fear and began to cry. Then suddenly the rope released, and I plunged, screaming, through the air toward the men below me.

A sudden jolt left me hanging above Ted's raging face. He screamed at me, "Stop your crying! You are not dead yet!"

The harness grabbed around my waist, and I felt my body rising again into the air. Looking down at the men below, I waited for the drop that I knew was coming. I whimpered, afraid. I did not want to fall, but the inevitable was near. The tension of the rope that lifted me released, and I felt myself plunging, once again, toward the angry face below.

Ted's face appeared even more terrifying as he shouted, "You're not dead yet!"

I have no memory of whether it was three or even more times I was dropped by the rope. I only remember going limp, numb, and silent, which must have proven to Ted that I was now dead.

The stronghold that Ted had on me stemmed not only from this immense fear that I had of him but also from the trauma bond with him that was cemented through events like this.[1] I learned that if I did as I was told and performed well, I was less likely to be hurt and punished.

The barbarity of Ted's depraved acts continued to impact my life until I was almost nine. It was then that my family moved away to the third church my dad would pastor.

---

[1] "Trauma bonding is a psychological response to abuse. The person experiencing abuse may develop sympathy for the abusive person, which becomes reinforced by cycles of abuse, followed by remorse. . . . Stockholm syndrome is one type of trauma bonding." (Lois Zoppi, "Trauma Bonding Explained," MedicalNewsToday.com, May 25, 2023, https://www.medicalnewstoday.com/articles/trauma-bonding.)

The Destroyer, Part I: What Happened?

Thankfully, Ted's access to me was spread out, with long gaps in between, during the eight years we lived in this idyllic Minnesota town.

However, the unpredictability of never knowing if I would be in Ted's grip again only increased my anxiety. His sinister abuse over time affected me mentally, emotionally, physically, spiritually, and sexually. The darker Ted's imagination became, the more venomous his performances were on his victims. I was not the only one Ted abused. There were times I was with other frightened children, and there were other adults who had been seduced to take part in his dark reality.

I became hypervigilant and withdrawn. I escaped by entering an inner world that I created, climbing a pine tree in our front yard, and knocking on another tree to invite my imaginary friends to come out and play with me. As I got older, I spent time with friends down the block or with my best friend at her home. I stayed away from my house as much as I could, for fear that the monstrous form of Ted might appear at our door. By third grade, I had already removed myself from being emotionally present, even in my own home.

In addition to the fear he wielded, Ted lured and charmed me with a side of him that could make me feel special and even chosen.

Shortly after I turned six, I remember Ted taking me to a pond where he had a rowboat. He took me for a ride out on the pond, and I felt special that he had chosen me to come with him. When the ride ended, he showed me some baby goats that had been born some weeks earlier. He told me to pick one and I could hold it. I played with this adorable little goat for the rest of the day.

That evening, we were outside when he took the goat from me. He held back the head of the baby goat and slit its throat in front of me. Watching the blood pour from its neck, I again froze—in shock, unable to move.

The very stench of evil permeated Ted. He was more than a pedophile. Ted had an insatiable, unquenchable hunger for evil, and I—and his victims—paid the price for Ted's lasciviousness.

The impact of Ted's violence on my life created living nightmares that I had to find a way to survive—and I did survive. Being able to dissociate allowed me to live in two worlds: the normal, everyday events of my life and the hidden world of Ted's secret hell.

When I eventually entered therapy in my late twenties, I had locked away, deep inside me, these details from my past. I did not have a clue about what I would face, but I knew I needed help with understanding why I got so angry. It would be six years, in and out of therapy with various therapists, before the circumstances of my life would feel safe enough for my past nightmares to emerge.

It erupted one day when my husband, David, thought it might be a promising idea to go back to the town where I'd spent my early years. At this point in time, I had no idea what I had repressed for most of my life.

We made the journey to Minnesota, and I showed him around town, telling him about all the lovely people I had known and showing him where they lived. At a restaurant near a lake where I used to swim, we had lunch with my favorite family of all, the Erikssons. We laughed and shared wonderful memories. My husband and I had the most pleasant of days.

As we were saying our goodbyes in the parking lot before returning to my sister's home fifty miles away, a thought drifted into my mind. I asked my friends, "Do you know where Ted Larkin's farmhouse is and how we might drive by there before we head back to my sister's?" Of course, they knew and gave us detailed directions.

We said our goodbyes, and my husband and I set off to make this final stop. On the way there, David and I shared about how good it was to be with my friends and what a lovely day this had been. My heart was full of joy and gratitude.

As we turned down the final gravel road, we neared the house that Ted had once lived in. David pulled over to the side of the road across from the house, and I said, "Yup, that's the house." I had no other reaction to it, other than knowing it was a familiar house. I was ready to head back to my sister's home.

Then David said what would become a turning point in my life, "Let's drive into the driveway."

I emphatically replied, "No! That would be trespassing. We cannot do that."

Assuring me it would be okay, David turned in and began to drive toward the back of the house. Suddenly, everything shifted into slow motion as every inch of the wheels took us closer to the back of the house. As the car turned, my eyes seemed drawn to the back door. It was then that I experienced an unexpected and out-of-the-ordinary reaction.

Panicking, I began clawing at the window, screaming, "Get me out of here! Get me out of here!"

My heart was pounding. I could not catch my breath and felt I might die. I was in a full-blown panic attack. I had never experienced one before, but it was to be the first of many to come.

David turned the car around and quickly exited the driveway. He drove down the road to a place where he could pull over. He patiently waited until I could begin to calm myself as he comforted me. He assured me that I was safe and that we would head back to my sister's house. On the return drive, we talked about what had happened, but I could make little sense of my reaction. I only knew that when I saw the back door, I felt and knew that what was inside that door was evil.

I called my therapist and told him what had occurred, His response was, "Well, we need to know what happened behind that back door." This began four years of intense therapy to face what had happened to me as a child.

I entered into the hardest work I have ever done. I did this because I believed that if I faced what had happened to me and had the courage to walk through the pain, I would come out free on the other side—no longer a hostage chained to my past.

The Destroyer, Part I: What Happened?

It did take great courage to face the reality of my past. In fact, it took all my courage to face the intense flashbacks, the night terrors, and the physical and emotional memories that were crushing and demoralizing. But I was determined not to give up until I was no longer terrified of my past, the phantom of Ted and his power over me—even though I knew by this point that he had died years earlier.

The power of indoctrination that Ted had over me was not easily dismantled, but with the help of my therapist, I took it apart piece by piece.

And finally, the day did arrive when I was no longer Ted's victim.

It was a beautiful spring day, and I had returned to my Minnesota hometown for a funeral to honor a woman who had loved me well as a child.

Before attending the funeral, I took some time to go to Ted Larkin's grave site. Finding it, I stood in silence for a time. I then began pacing back and forth on his grave. I moved from his headstone to the end of his plot, until I found my voice to speak my words aloud.

"Ted, it is a beautiful day. The sky is blue, the birds are singing, the early signs of spring are beginning to show. I am here and I am alive. I survived. I do not know where you are, except that I know your decaying body is beneath me, and I am walking on top of your grave. You did not destroy me. You did not win. I won this fight to live my life—the life you wanted to destroy."

As I continued to process the debris of what had happened to me as a child, I knew I did not want to carry the emotional weight of Ted and his abuse. It took a lot of time, but eventually I was able to say, "I forgive you. I release you, and I will live my life as the person I know myself to be. I am good."

Reflection on My Story

Whenever a traumatic event or a report of abuse is revealed, our immediate response is often, "What happened?"

Our need to know is more than mere curiosity. It has more to do with wanting to understand how this could have happened and what kind of a person could have done such a thing.

For the survivor of such atrocities, it is important to express openly what happened. I often relay to my family and friends that putting the pieces of my past together was like putting together a million-piece puzzle without being able to look at the picture on the box. Yet with each piece that fit together, I began to have the answers that slowly put my life back in order.

I have always been tenacious in facing what I discovered in my life. I never gave up. I lived by the motto, "I am not doing therapy to get a life; I am doing therapy and life."

However, no two people who have endured traumatic events will deal with their abuse in the same way. It is important to honor each one's conviction of what they believe they need in their process. There is no "right" or "wrong" way to recover. It must be the unique way of each individual. For some, healing can occur within months; for others, it is a prolonged journey. Yet the goal is the same for all: face the truth, honor the process, do not give up, and know that your liberation is near.

I can honestly say that, as horrible as my experiences were as a child and as horrible as my quite painful recovery was for me, I do not regret one bit of it. The passage that I was required to walk to take my life back out of the hands of the ones who wished to destroy it was more than worth it.

What Is Your Story?

I encourage you not to say to yourself, "Wow, my story is not as bad as Faith's. I may not have any trauma or abuse in my background—at least, not like what happened to her."

Trauma can occur from the moderate to the most extreme events in your life. A scary situation on the playground, a horror movie, a painful injury, surgery, or death in the family are examples of events that can leave a film of trauma over your life. Parents, relatives, teachers, clergy, or any person in authority could frighten, intimidate, and do emotional, physical, and psychological harm.

These moments in time are often placed on the back shelves of our subconscious until we remember or decide to face what we may have minimized or dismissed as "not a big deal."

Do not judge your past situations. Explore them and observe them with curiosity to see if there is anything from your past that might still be affecting or controlling how you react to circumstances in your everyday life.

Your story holds a prominent place in your life, and when it is valued and heard, your personal freedom is a step closer.

Can you recall a frightening, sad, or embarrassing event in your life as a child, teenager, or adult? Sometimes, even getting lost from a parent can be a trauma-inducing event.

How did you react?

How did you deal with what had happened?

Is there a correlation from a past event (or events) to how you may react in situations you face today?

Share Your Story

Disclosing your story may be too difficult for you to consider—but if you have the right person to listen, as you confide in them, you are likely to find great relief at the conclusion of your story.

If you come to realize that your fear has increased or you are having physical or emotional symptoms that affect your daily routine, please seek out a professional who specializes in trauma, abuse, and PTSD. You deserve to be not only heard but supported through the process of overcoming what never should have occurred in your life.

Whatever your story is, honor it, respect it, learn from it, and overthrow the lie embedded within your story by seeking the truth that is there to be found.

5

THE RESTORER

"Faith, I'm all done with the dishes—what would you like to do now?" Mrs. Eriksson's kind voice rings through from the kitchen. Even at four years old, I can hear her gentle excitement at this chance to spend time with me. I'm certain she already knows what my answer will be.

Without any hesitation I exclaim, "Listen to *Peter and the Wolf*!"

I run into her living room and climb onto her gold-and-green-striped couch. It takes effort to lift my little legs up onto the couch cushion, surrounded by pillows embroidered with images of colorful flowers that match the footstool nearby. Everything in this room is magical. Oil paintings on the walls have a light above each one that brings the image to life. The thick carpet, perfectly vacuumed, embraces my stockinged feet, and the fragrance of clean, combined with the smell of something I have never smelled before, makes me feel special.

"Well then, let's do this," Mrs. Eriksson says. She walks over to the cabinet stereo, lifts the lid, and opens the sliding wooden cabinet door to the side. A display of neatly placed and ordered albums appears. She thumbs her way down to find the exact album among the many records Mr. Eriksson has collected. She carefully removes *the* record, holding it ever so gently on the edges. Placing it on the turntable, she puts the needle onto its edge; soon it will start. She comes back to the couch where I am waiting just as the orchestra begins to play the melody that tells me the story is about to begin. I already know what is coming next. The man on the record will begin telling which instrument will be each animal or person in the story.

She puts her arm around me and I snuggle in close to her. As much as I love this musical story of *Peter and the Wolf*, it terrifies me to listen to it unless Mrs. Eriksson is here to move in close to. When the three loud horns play (that's the wolf), I press in even tighter against her as I shiver, letting her know that this is the scary part. When the wolf eats the duck, Mrs. Eriksson says, "It's okay. The duck will be okay."

I am safe, protected, loved, and cherished. A feeling I always feel when I am with her, especially in her house. I love being at her house, just the two of us. When my parents need someone to watch me, she is my favorite person of all to be with. Sometimes we watch *As the World Turns* as she irons her laundry. She uses all® brand detergent to wash her clothes, and the smell makes me feel like I am somewhere magical.

Mrs. Eriksson never gets angry or frustrated with me. Her patience and smile tell me that I am safe in her presence... always.

I remember in great detail Mrs. Eriksson's upriver home on the Mississippi. Years later, she and her husband would build another home, downriver from this one. Each home held many wonderful memories for me of good food, comfort, safety, luxury, and love.

I still hold dear the beautiful birthday and Christmas gifts she gave me. Perfectly wrapped with a big bow, beneath the wrappings the box often cradled a beautiful new dress that I would treasure wearing until it no longer fit me.

One long-lasting result of my relationship with Mrs. Eriksson is that I *love* funeral homes.

"Why in the world?" you might ask. Because Mrs. Eriksson's husband was a mortician, and there were many times I was with Mrs. Eriksson at the funeral home. In fact, while their new house was being built, they lived in an apartment above the funeral home. I had the chance to stay with them a couple of times at this apartment, while my parents were off on one of their ministry conference trips.

At the time, I was taking piano lessons, so of course I had to practice. Downstairs in the chapel, behind the drapes, sat the piano, beside an organ that was played at memorial services.

One time, I remember skipping down the stairs from the apartment to the chapel. There, in the chapel, sat a casket with its lid open. As I passed by it to get to the piano behind the curtain, I tiptoed up to the casket and waved at the man lying there and said, "Hello!" I then went on and practiced at the piano. When I had completed my half hour, I carried my piano books past the man in the casket, waved again, and said, "Goodbye!"

I had no fear of being in the funeral home. I delighted in walking into the room where the caskets were for sale. Each wooden or metal box was artfully lined with satin. They looked beautiful and magical to my five-year-old self.

How was it possible that I could feel free and safe in a funeral home that represented death to the world, while at the same time I was being abused by villainous people who terrified me?

The Erikssons were light, love, goodness, and protection to me. The funeral home represented this as much as did their beautiful homes, embracing me with loving security. It was the love of the Erikssons who owned the funeral home that created this love and life. The corrupt people in my world were the ones with whom I experienced death.

Over the years, I would see Mrs. Eriksson from time to time. Her face always lit up when she saw me. Her smile would expand across her face, and I would feel like I was at home. She had become a sort of surrogate grandmother to me. My actual grandmother lived clear across the country, and I only saw her once every four years.

As previously mentioned, David and I returned to my idyllic hometown later in my life. Of course, I wanted to see Mrs. Eriksson on my visit there. I made the arrangements with her daughter, since Mr. Eriksson had passed. It was then that I learned that Mrs. Eriksson had returned to live in the upstairs apartment above the funeral home.

When David and I arrived, I was greeted by Mrs. Eriksson's daughter and son-in-law. Her daughter went to help Mrs. Eriksson down the stairs as I stood at the bottom, watching for her to appear. Within a few minutes I saw an elegantly regal, perfectly coiffed, white-haired woman descending the stairs with her cane.

As she neared the end of her descent, she saw me and exclaimed, "Oh, my Faith!"

Reaching the last step, she enveloped me in her arms. Her loving smile spread across her face, and her love poured out over me once again. Then we were off to lunch at the restaurant by the lake where David and I would share the next two hours in joyful conversation with Mrs. Eriksson and her daughter and son-in-law.

Our time together that day filled my heart to overflowing. With laughter, hugs, and goodbyes, David and I headed off to our last stop: the farmhouse of Ted Larkin where I was about to experience the key trigger that would unlock a past I had repressed for thirty years.

Just a few years later, I would return for Mrs. Eriksson's funeral. She was once again elegantly dressed in a mauve dress, resting on a slightly deeper shade of mauve satin that lined her casket. She was at peace. I grieved but at the same time celebrated this precious soul for the saving impact she had had on my life.

By the time I attended Mrs. Eriksson's memorial service, I had overcome many of my past demons. As I mentioned in the previous chapter, I also visited Ted's grave site and released to him my forgiveness for what he had done to me.

This visit completed the circle that had begun so long ago as a child. I no longer feared the destroyer, for on this day I honored the restorer in my life, Mrs. Eriksson, whose love chased away the big bad wolf.

Reflection on My Story

What I did not understand as a child, I came to grasp as an adult. There were those who abused me, but when Mrs. Eriksson and I listened to *Peter and the Wolf*, the comfort she gave by holding me tight during the scary parts unknowingly helped me work through some of my unspoken trauma. By experiencing the love of Mrs. Eriksson, I discovered someone who would protect me—even when there had been many times, with more to come, where I had not been protected.

Did she protect me from my abusers? No, she did not know there were horrifying things happening to me. But her love for me penetrated my heart and somehow instilled hope and the assurance that whatever I was going through, there would be a time when I would be back in the presence of Mrs. Eriksson's love. My world was not all bad. It held the truth of both good and evil.

In hindsight, I realize I was experiencing the reality of overcoming evil with good. The goodness within Mrs. Eriksson was a gift that was instrumental in helping me to defeat the dark cruelty that had been done to me. The power of love and goodness was a force so bright that it penetrated the darkness I faced then. It is a force of change that I use to this day.

What Is Your Story?

Who was the person who was a restorer or positive influence in your life?

What did they do or say that made a difference and a positive impact on your life?

What characteristics changed in you because of their influence?

Share Your Story

When you share with another person about someone who made a restorative impact on your life, you are not only honoring the person who touched your life, but your words stand as a reminder that you were not alone on life's journey. Your memory becomes a blanket of truth, hope, and wisdom to wrap around yourself to withstand challenging days.

6

It Will Be Over Soon

I feel the bite of the chilling autumn wind penetrate my skin. Increasing with each gust, the bitter cold shakes the decaying leaves in the canopy above me. In the coal black of the night, I catch glimpses of leaves dropping to the ground. Their dry crunch beneath my feet holds me rooted in one spot, for fear that I might make a sound that will awaken the dark things in the woods that I have been told will come drag me away.

Ted Larkin and his "friends" have freely taken me from the caretaker's home where my family left me while they attend another conference. Ted, being related to the caretaker, found it possible to access me whenever I landed for a few days in the home of his cousin. Ted had left me alone in scary places before. I could tell he enjoyed leaving me alone, because he always laughed with a smirk on his face when he would say, "Do as you're told. Don't move. Obey."

I am alone in this strange place, unable to see my surroundings. The colder I become, the more my fear increases. I've been told to stay here, to not move, or bad things will happen to me. Bad things *are* happening to me, and my imagination increases with images of the monsters that are waiting for me.

I don't remember how old I was when I first found a way to disappear from these terrifying outings. When I was very young, I imagined that the bear that Ted told me was in the woods would come and eat me. I also imagined that bad monsters would come hurt me with their claws. The woods were not safe, and when Ted instructed me to be silent—to not make even the slightest sound—I obeyed. To defy Ted meant there would be consequences that I knew I did not want to experience.

Having seen his rage explode at others, having felt the pinch of his fingers on my shoulder and skin, having been forced to climb into a box with spiders, and many even more outrageous punishments, I quickly learned to be silent and do as I was told.

But there came a time when I found a magical entrance to disappear from the overwhelming thoughts running through my mind. It happened when I began to speak aloud to myself, ever so softly, "It will be over soon . . ."

It did not matter if it was day or night. If painful, scary, or yucky things were happening to me, I began repeating these five words, "It will be over soon. It will be over soon. It will be over soon." And then I would go *away*—far, far away from the cold, the terror, and the nightmarish possibilities of what would happen to me if I disobeyed.

From that time forward, whenever Ted Larkin found ways to gain access to me, I used my magical words to escape from whatever he told me to do. What I did not know then was that my magical words would continue to take me away from the terrifying things I would face in my future.

Each year, my parents decided where we were going for our vacation. Sometimes it meant going back East where our extended family lived; other times it was to spend a week or two in a rental cabin on the lake. It didn't matter where we went or what time of year we vacationed: when our family car was packed with lunches in the cooler, ready to head out, we would all be excited and eager to go—all, that is, except for my mom. She would eventually come out, get in the car, and in her panic and anger, say, "I can't go. I know I have forgotten something. You all go without me."

"Honey, it doesn't matter," my dad would calmly say. "Everything is good. You can go—of course you are going."

This only escalated my mom's response. "I don't want to go! The rest of you go. I'm staying home."

Each year, I would sit in the back seat with my siblings, watching this familiar drama unfold. I would press my back into the seat, wondering if our vacation was going to end before it even began. As my mom's voice got louder and Dad did whatever he could to calm her, I felt trapped. The all-too-familiar feeling of fear rose within me. I wanted to get out of the car, but couldn't, so it was then that I would speak my magic words to myself: "It will be over soon." The intensity of my fear would subside, and I'd catch my breath with a deep inhale.

As I repeated, "It will be over soon, it will be over soon, it will be over soon," in time my dad would talk my mom down. He would then pray aloud in the car for traveling mercies, and Mom would say she would go, Dad would start the car, and we would finally be off.

There were other times I used this magical phrase to escape a situation where I felt powerless and afraid.

I was a clock-watcher in school. If I felt frightened or threatened in a class, I would begin clicking off the minutes while repeating to myself, "It will be over soon." My phrase gave me the assurance that my anxiety would end once I was allowed to leave the confinement of the classroom. This became my pattern throughout all my years of education.

Sometimes the minutes would click off slowly—painfully slowly—other times the minutes moved by more quickly. Either way, I had years of experience to know that in time the weight of my fears would subside. The passage of time brought an end to my suffering—or so I thought.

Years later I would discover that the passage of time only brought temporary relief. My mantra, "It will be over soon," simply carried me to an ending but not a resolution. I had believed that the movement of the hands on the clock would make all the difference for my safety and life. I had believed that once time passed, the terrible things that had happened would also disappear. Instead, I carried my suffering, fears, and memories into the future, not realizing that the passage of time did not allow me to leave them behind.

◦∽

It had been thirty-six hours of hard labor. My first child. Every nurse reassured me that this was normal. My labor pains increased with each passing hour. Much of the time I was left alone in my hospital room to face these waves of torture. I did my best to breathe through each tightening grip and was determined to obey the two programmed messages left me by Ted and my mother.

Ted would say, "Do not make a sound, be very still." This would keep me safe.

Mom would say, "When giving birth, I never let on that I was in pain. I wasn't going to give anyone *that* satisfaction. I held in my screams." The implication was that this somehow made her a strong woman—a message I internalized and one that held a stoic and substantive meaning.

I did my best to follow these internalized commands, but somewhere around the forty-second hour of labor, I unknowingly grabbed a fistful of my hair and yanked it out, at the same time grabbing a plate and flinging it across the room. I screamed at the top of my lungs, "I cannot do this anymore! Make . . . it . . . stop!"

A nurse came running into my room and told me not to shout. I was sobbing by then and begged her to make it all go away. I was being tortured, and I simply wanted it to end.

She said, "Okay, let's get this baby born!"

I don't know exactly what occurred next, but she began working with me. I am not sure where she had been during the earlier hours. Perhaps there were too many other babies being born and not enough nurses. All I wanted was help, but in a small midwestern town with a modest hospital to care for a surrounding community, perhaps limited care was to be expected.

Within a few hours, I was taken into the delivery room where we waited for the doctor to arrive. I remember little of the three hours during which this nurse helped me to bring my child into this world. I do remember the sound of her first cry, the nurses saying, "It's a girl!" and seeing the hands of the clock straight up at 6:00 p.m. It was over. My daughter had arrived.

The pain had not ended quickly over those two-plus days. In fact, the pain I endured overrode all other thoughts including, *It will be over soon*, but in time the pain ended as I held my baby girl in my arms.

Six or eight weeks after the birth of my daughter, I went to see the doctor for my postnatal checkup. The nurse escorted me to the exam room and asked the basic questions and took my vitals. The doctor was then left alone in the room with me as he did my internal exam. I stayed relaxed, even trusting this man who had delivered my firstborn just weeks before—until his finger began to stimulate me inappropriately. Even though his violation of me was for a few brief moments, I froze.

I did not move. I stared at the ceiling. I did not make a sound. I began to hear in my mind, *It will be over soon. It will be over soon.* I went far away and do not remember how I left the doctor's office or even how I got home that day.

As for how these experiences affected my relationships with friends and dating, I acquiesced to what they wanted to do. I had been taught to be silent and to serve. I had learned through experience that submitting without argument was the safer path. Even when my relationships had proven to be safe, my past encounters lived on through a current narrative that had been embedded deep within my subconscious years earlier.

My personality is that of a caring, considerate person who enjoys giving to others. This being true, it was hard for me to discern the difference between who I naturally was and the part of me that gave in to others due to my past trauma. The very traits that made me a compassionate person were the qualities that were exploited to control me.

This is not to say that I did not have fun in life. I most certainly did enjoy the friends I made throughout the years as well as my family and the great adventures that came our way. But upon reflection, I realize I was okay with doing whatever the other person preferred to do. I found myself unaware of my automatic responses that had been integrated into my day-to-day life. I yielded my will to others because of my conditioning and my belief that life was unsafe and must be survived. This way of interacting with others was so natural to me that I never questioned it.

I found that keeping things low-key was to my advantage. Escalation or confrontation became an immediate threat. I had learned as a child how to read facial expressions, observing even the most subtle nuances or shifts in a person's character. I could intuitively *feel* if a person had the potential to harm me or not.

What I did not have the ability to do was to use my voice to stop a potential predator. I did not believe I had the right to set a boundary. Indeed, I did not even know how to set a boundary. Saying the word *Stop!* was dangerous, yelling for help meant impending punishment, and it was impossible for me to run away when I was emotionally frozen, suspended in time.

I had discovered long ago that I could use appeasement. I could become submissive with my potential villain, use respectful politeness to deescalate the situation. As an adult, I would learn that these were all fawning traits that I had used in the hope of being able to escape the person who I believed might harm me.[2]

It took me years of working on the origins of my fear and survival mechanisms before I eventually healed. I found ways to empower myself and find my voice in threatening situations. Over time, I came to believe that I was free from ever being intimidated again. But I was wrong.

---

[2] "Fawning" is a term used in psychology to describe a trauma response that involves consistently abandoning one's own needs to serve others in order to avoid conflict, criticism, or disapproval.

Imagine my surprise when, just this year, I found myself intimidated by a hardworking man named Gabe whom my husband and I had hired, along with his team, to do some seasonal yard cleanup.

Gabe's stature was tall and strong, and he was extremely friendly—an in-command, take-charge person. He was exactly the type of man we wanted for the job, but it was how he approached me that set off my internal alarms. Instead of asking or requesting something of me, he would use his smooth and somewhat seductive voice to order me to do something.

He would say, "Walk with me, I want to show you what I did." At his command, I found myself following him without hesitation. He would explain what he was going to do next and why he had done some jobs that my husband had not requested. It all appeared to be a good work ethic, but I felt myself becoming robotic around him.

The second day he came with his crew, I felt more hesitant to be near him, and I judged myself for feeling the way that I did. *Something must be wrong with me.* Gabe appeared to be respectful, but his commanding style and need to be in control inhibited my ability to voice the possible healthy responses I heard running through my head. I found myself unable to say them aloud to Gabe.

I recognized I had become quieter and passive, pulling back and acquiescing to whatever he wanted. It did not matter whether it was his command to come at once to see his work or his asking for my approval and affirmation of him. I felt his demands on me, and this set off old fear responses.

My husband, David, also observed Gabe's take-charge approach in the way he overrode David's directions for the job. David could also see that Gabe's interactions were affecting me. As we discussed the situation, I began to understand just how caught off guard I was by the fear that rose up within me around Gabe. I had returned to my coping skill of fawning, without even realizing I was doing so.

I used to judge myself harshly whenever my old coping skills surfaced or I found myself frozen or triggered in a way I had assured myself would never happen again.

But today I know there is no guarantee for a "one-and-done" in healing. The scars of my past are tender to the touch. Are they healed? Yes. But I can feel how that area in my life is different if something brushes up against it or touches it with a direct hit.

However, these times of impact have become an opportunity for me to discover what has been repressed, ignored, or disguised. I have come to see these times as a chance to discover areas where I have not fully shaken off the particles of debris that have inserted themselves into my responses. To ignore the obvious never actually erases the truth that it offers. I must decide if I will face it or store it away for another day.

My new response, learned from choosing to heal and recover, is, *Faith, the sooner you deal with this, the better it will be for you. It is not going away. It will 'be over soon' the sooner you face what you are feeling—and deal with what has surfaced.*

I no longer avoid what I am hesitant to face about myself but choose to get to work. I take the first step by doing what I must to claim the freedom that awaits me at the end of this particular finish line. And yes, there will be other finish lines that I will continue to face and cross over in my life, but this is how I honor myself—by overcoming what should never have happened to me.

Reflection on My Story

This was a difficult chapter for me to write, because I saw more clearly how much I had accepted that what had happened to me was just a part of my life. I had come to view these experiences through my mind's eye, rather than through the feelings that I held in my innermost being.

I cried with the child who was so afraid in the woods and with the twenty-two-year-old who had been in agonizing labor for so long all alone and who'd been betrayed by her doctor whom she had come to trust.

My heart opened at a new level to the suffering that over time I had come to neutralize, perhaps in an attempt to distance myself from what had occurred throughout my life.

My lifelong experiences are more real to me now because a new light of truth has illuminated what I went through emotionally. It is here—even in the pain of feeling what I could not feel then—that I find further healing.

WHAT IS YOUR STORY?

How would you describe events in your life that were frightening or painful?

Have you dismissed hard and painful experiences in life as not that important, or as something that you just have to get over, because "that's life"?

Is there anything that may be keeping you from facing some experiences you had in your past?

SHARE YOUR STORY

Can you imagine sharing with someone the things you have never shared with anyone before?

Even if you have shared your story, did you share it openly and honestly? Or was it shared in passing, spoken with humor, or at a time when you may have had too much to drink? Did you end up feeling serious regret for sharing as you did?

To face the truth of your experience—your story—honor yourself by doing the following:

First, be *ready* to share your story.

Second, find the right person—a trustworthy person—with whom to share your story.

Third, be honest with the person as to how you feel before sharing your story, during the time you're sharing your story, and after you have shared your story.

In doing so, you will have taken the most courageous step toward being free of what you were never meant to carry alone.

7

BETRAYED

Author's Note: *Betrayal appears in both blatant and subtle ways, often when we least expect it. The carriers of betrayal can be family members, friends, coworkers, religious communities, employers or employees, medical professionals, scammers, or even strangers. The most painful betrayals occur when the ones we have trusted never to hurt us are the ones who shatter our hearts.*

At four years of age, when adults asked me, "Faith, what do you want to be when you grow up?" my immediate and enthusiastic response was always, "A bride!"

Having been asked to be a flower girl in two weddings that year, I'm certain that my answer was swayed by the fact that brides had special parties at which they (and every other woman) got to wear beautiful dresses. I continued to carry the dream of being a bride as I played with my favorite bride doll, given to me by my Aunt Dot on my sixth Christmas. Imagining a day in a beautiful gown became my personal Cinderella story that would somehow carry me away from everything that terrified me in my young life.

Through the years I wondered, *Is there such a thing as Prince Charming for me in the world?*

Then, at the age of nineteen, I believed I had met him. I was incredibly naïve in many areas of life, having been raised by a dad who was a minister, along with a performance-oriented and rule-following mother. My upbringing stunted me from learning how the world around me existed. I knew there were bad people and good people in the world, but I knew nothing of human behavior and what to watch out for.

At the age of nineteen, I was genuinely afraid of living my life. I was fearful of continuing education; I felt rejected as a person and saw myself as an unacceptable human being—a failure. Fear was a constant—a camouflage that hid from me childhood abuse that my mind had purposefully filed away. My constant thoughts dictated messages of failure, punishment, and rejection.

With little to no confidence that I had any intelligence (actually I believed I was intellectually poverty-stricken), I picked a business school in Rapid City, South Dakota, and decided to take classes in the travel industry. Was this what I really wanted to do? Not really, but it was *something*, and it played into my fantasy of finding a way to escape from life.

My parents drove me to Rapid City a week before classes began, because they had plans to be on vacation the following week. Unable to move into the dorm early, a friend of mine offered to let me stay with her and her sister's family for that week. I was dropped off at their home, said goodbye to my dad and mom, and began the countdown until I could move onto campus.

My first day of class never arrived. In those five short days, the owner of the house swept me off my feet—or at least, this is what I thought was happening. I can honestly say that I do not remember much about that week, except that he was always there at the house, unless he was at meetings with his salespeople. His wife, a professor at another college in Rapid City, was rarely home, and I saw her only a couple of times during the five days I was there.

My Prince Charming's name was Grayson, and because eating at home was a rare occurrence, this meant that whoever was at the house during meal times would eat out together at a restaurant—breakfast, lunch, and dinner. My friend worked during the day, and so this left me with Grayson and his eight-year-old son, TK, to have meals together—if TK wasn't with his friends or mother.

Restaurants were a rare treat at my home because a minister's income did not allow such extravagant extras except on very rare occasions. Eating out for every meal was a different reality. It all felt indulgent and exciting.

One afternoon, it was only Grayson and me at home to do lunch. I suddenly felt grown up and special, which drew me even more to this person who was taking me on these out-of-the-ordinary adventures.

Grayson told me to order whatever I wanted. I couldn't believe that I had this choice. I had never had steak in a restaurant before—or anywhere, for that matter. The entire meal captivated me, while at the same time, unbeknownst to me, Grayson was captivated by me.

I was unaware that Grayson was pursuing me with his long conversations and taking me to wonderful places to eat. It never occurred to me that a married man, fourteen years my senior, had any reason to be interested in me. But I was wrong. Over the brief time I was in his home, it became clear that Grayson had taken an interest in me. He saw me and made me feel special.

On the fourth evening of being at the home of my friend's family, I was downstairs in the family room. Grayson came down to be with me and without hesitation leaned in and kissed me. His hands began to go further and quickly made it clear that he wanted to have sex with me. I told him, "No, I can't do this with you." He agreed and left me alone.

What neither of us knew at the time was that my friend, who lived there with her sister and Grayson, had seen what he was doing through an outdoor window. She of course told her sister—Grayson's wife—what she had seen. They both thought that *I* was the problem—the betrayer in all of this.

Fortunately, I left the next day because my week had thankfully come to an end. Grayson drove me to the campus, but on the way over he told me that he loved me, wanted to marry me, and was going to divorce his wife. His announcement was overwhelming, terrifying, and thrilling, all at the same time. Someone wanted me and was ready to take me away from a place I did not want to be. I was on the brink of facing one of my biggest fears: starting school the next day. Now, here I was being rescued at the last minute. I felt relief.

I stayed for only one night in my dorm room. Classes were to start the next day. Grayson had already talked to me about not starting business college. He said that in the morning he would come with me to withdraw me from school.

As promised, he was there, and we went into the office together. We sat down with someone in administration, and Grayson did most of the talking.

The man sitting at his desk, looking across at both of us, turned to me. "Are you wanting to withdraw from attending here?"

I nodded, "Yes, I want to withdraw."

He turned to Grayson and said, "All of this concerns me for Faith. Things are happening so fast, and the age difference is also concerning."

Grayson assured him that we were in love and that he would take good care of me.

I packed up my things in my dorm room and eagerly left the school on a hot August day. On November 22 of that year, I was married to Grayson.

It wasn't the big wedding I had always imagined, but I told myself it didn't matter and that I didn't really care. I was going to marry someone who adored me and wanted to spend his life with me. I wore a simple gown that I chose with a small cap veil. My parents, Grayson's parents, and a few of Grayson's friends were in attendance—a total of eight or ten, including Grayson and myself.

My dad could not marry us because Grayson had been divorced. So a Lutheran minister joined us together, and then it was off to a steak house where we all had a good meal. I don't remember much about that evening. I was married, I would be cared for, and I would care for him.

One early spring afternoon, four months into our marriage, Grayson, in his gentle and affectionate voice, said he wanted to talk to me. We were in our bedroom, and as I sat on the edge of the bed, I wondered what was so important for him to need to speak with me. Had I done something wrong?

What he was about to say to me would become the single most devastating betrayal I have faced in life.

Grayson's first words were, "I love you; you know that."

I nodded yes.

He continued, "I love apples. They are my favorite fruit to eat, but sometimes I enjoy eating a peach, or a pear, or some other fruit."

I responded, "Okay, what are you saying?" I literally thought in my head, *Is he telling me he likes fruit salad? Why is he being so serious talking about fruit?*

Grayson came closer to me to explain what my naïveté had no understanding or experience of, nor any known category for which to make sense of this fruit story.

He softened his voice, filling it with deep affection, and continued, "Faith, I love you. You are my favorite. Like apples, you are my favorite fruit; but there are times when I would enjoy someone else, like I enjoy other kinds of fruit."

Slowly, the reality of his words flooded over me with a crashing force of heaviness I had never experienced before. I could not breathe. I felt my chest caving in with pain that felt like it had arrived to destroy my very existence.

A foreign substance welled up inside me, nauseating me. My head was spinning with feelings of confusion, anger, and rejection, all combined into a ball of incomprehension that rushed my brain and flooded my body.

The pain I felt was all-consuming. My body no longer felt attached to me, and a tunnel of blackness pulled me into its void. I could no longer hear clearly or focus on what my eyes were seeing. Sixteen years later, I would learn that I was dissociating in order to survive what I believed to be true in that moment: that I would not live through this experience.

I don't recall what happened next. I remember protesting and saying, "No!" but Grayson assured me nothing would change his love for me. I remember crying—feeling shattered and undone—until sleep drew me into nothingness.

None of Grayson's fruit story made any sense to me. I did not know that marriage was anything other than sacred and faithful. This is what I had been taught, and I was all in. My husband was not.

Betrayal had taken up residency in our home, and I believed I had no choice but to allow it to remain there. My ability to see that I had a choice had been erased years before as a child. I had married for life, and I was trapped. Grayson was in charge, so I would need to learn how to navigate a world I knew nothing about.

In the years to follow, I became inured to his lecherous predations. At the same time, I learned excellent business skills by working under his giftedness as a successful entrepreneur and businessman. I was living in two realities.

It would be another seven and a half years before I found my voice and the courage to tell Grayson, "I won't do this anymore." That empowered moment happened after he informed me that he wanted to live with me for six months out of the year and have his newfound girlfriend live with him the other six months of the year—in *our* home.

I began divorce proceedings. The nightmare needed to end.

Reflection on My Story

Grayson has passed. He had two additional marriages after his marriage to me.

Grayson and I had a daughter together, to whom he relinquished all parental rights when I divorced him. The emotional pain he inflicted affected the next generation, but my daughter stands as a beacon of light that life is good and the legacy of pain can be broken. By living her life and loving her family as it was meant to be loved, she is living proof of this.

My daughter and I attended Grayson's funeral. I felt little to nothing as I reflected on the eight years of pain and chaos as well as the many dark experiences Grayson had left imprinted on my life through which I'd had to work. I had faced my pain in therapy and had come to an understanding of how I could have allowed someone to treat me the way I had been treated.

As I stood at his casket, looking at him lying there, I thought, *I have forgiven you, Grayson, because I do not want to carry the burden of pain and hate. I am thankful for two things that came out of our marriage. Most importantly, our daughter. Secondly, learning from you how to become a successful entrepreneur.*

I have learned that healing from life's painful experiences is rarely a one-and-done, or "just move on," or "just get over it." Most painful experiences come off in layers, over many years.

I discovered this to be true, once again, while writing this chapter. I came into a fuller grasp of what I had missed out on, what I had endured, and how it affected my life. This chapter in particular was meant to deepen my healing, and for this I am grateful.

What Is Your Story?

Betrayal is an ugly beast. It can slash our hearts, causing us to react in ways that we'd never think of behaving. If betrayal is not dealt with, it can take up residency within us, filling us with resentments, or causing us to withdraw or become controlling to protect ourselves.

So, what is your story?

Who has betrayed you?

How did you face and deal with the betrayal that was imposed upon you?

Share Your Story

Your story or stories of how you have been betrayed in life truly matter. Gossiping about how you were betrayed, however, is not sharing. What is the difference?

When you share your story, you are offering it to someone who will listen with compassion and insight. The listener is not there to fix anything but to support you, encourage you, and if they are wise, offer some helpful signposts along the way.

On the other hand, gossiping about your betrayal to anyone who will listen is just venting your emotions, and perhaps a way of making sure that others know just how bad the betrayer was. This may release some steam in the moment, but rarely will it move you closer to resolution.

Your pain is meant to be shared, but choose wisely the person or people with whom you share. The pain of betrayal deserves to be healed, not judged, and you deserve the utmost respect and care in the process.

When you find that person who will listen to you and hear the impact that betrayal has had on your life, this is honest and vulnerable sharing. When you can fully release what never should have happened to you—but did—forgiveness will come in time, and pain can be replaced with freedom and peace.

8

The Betrayer

Author's Note: *It is never easy to admit that I could hurt so many people in my life, but there can be no healing in withholding the truth—even if held tightly in a minuscule corner of my heart and mind. This particular chapter has been painful to write, but it is necessary for me to speak the truth of the following story. If truth is not spoken, dormant secrets will rise again and again, holding the potential to decay the soul.*

I had left my first husband, Grayson, had filed for divorce, and was in the early negotiations of dissolving our marriage. I was still running half of the business that we jointly held in two separate states. Part of my business included a gift shop, and it required that I attend three or more gift shows each year to order merchandise for the shop.

I had made the decision to attend a particular gift market in the Midwest. I headed there alone, with the plan of buying what I needed for the next season of sales, intending to head back home within a couple of days.

As I moved from one booth to another, each filled with enticing and interesting items meant to stop me in my tracks and make a sale, I came across an isolated booth displaying Western art prints. The artists were quite good, and their adeptness caught my attention. As I was flipping through some of the work that this company represented, the salesman approached.

"Hi there, pretty lady."

A bit taken aback, I smiled and said hello. I then asked him to tell me more about the prints. He gave details about the artists and the company. I intuitively knew these prints would sell nicely in my gift shop. I'm not sure when I decided to place an order; he was intent not only on making a sale, but it also became clear when he asked me to go out to dinner that he was a bit taken with me.

We had dinner together the following evening. One thing led to another, and not only did I buy the art he was selling; I also bought what he was personally selling. He was kind, a cowboy at heart and in appearance, and was nothing like Grayson. He felt safe, and it felt good to have someone interested in and attracted to me, after all the rejection I had tolerated while being married to Grayson.

His name was Jackson, and he wanted to continue to have contact with me. I told him that he could and began by extending my two-day trip an extra two days.

With calls and occasional visits, a romance began. I wasn't quite sure what I felt about him yet, but at this point in my life, if someone was interested in me, I could not say no to them. I still had no awareness of my past and how I had been taught and conditioned into this compliant behavior, not only by my childhood abusers and Grayson but by my religious upbringing as well.

I did truly come to care about Jackson. He was very different from other men I had dated. As the weeks progressed, so did our relationship, and I enjoyed taking the occasional sales trip with him.

Some months into our relationship, I joined him in Montana. He was visiting Glacier National Park and invited me to join him for a few days. I had visited this park several years back and had loved seeing its majestic beauty. I thought it would be a wonderful escape with someone who had begun to express that he cared a great deal about me.

While on this trip to Montana, Jackson turned to me one morning and, out of the blue, said, "Will you marry me?"

This being totally unexpected, a rush of messages began running through my mind. *Wait, what? It's too soon—I'm not sure about this. I did not see this coming. He is proposing to me now, here—was this a spur of the moment impulse, or did he plan it?*

I wanted desperately to say, "Wait a minute—let's talk about this," but what came out of my mouth instead was, "Yes."

I felt something deflate inside me. It wasn't how any woman should feel after just having been proposed to. My inability to be honest and the subconscious cues—over which I had no conscious control—silenced me, placing me into a compliant and obedient role once again. I had no conscious understanding as to why this was happening to me, but it was.

I had accepted his proposal, and I had been taught that my word was my bond. This was also part of being compliant and obedient. The exit door had now closed behind me.

Months later, we were married. Our wedding, once again, did not compare to the dream I had had as a child, teen, and adult, but I told myself—a second time—that it did not matter.

We found a preacher in South Dakota, and Jackson had two of his friends join us as witnesses. I remember nothing of the ceremony. I do remember withdrawing emotionally that evening, but I have no recall of what happened then or in the immediate days to follow. Knowing what I know now, I understand I slipped into survival mode, believing I had just lost myself.

Jackson moved into the home I had previously bought, and we settled into being a family. He adopted the daughter that Grayson and I had together, as Grayson had relinquished all rights as her father.

Our marriage lasted eight years, during which we had two additional daughters. Many factors on both of our parts played into the demise of our marriage, but the nail in the coffin came from my betrayal of Jackson and the marriage.

I had an affair—to be totally honest, I had more than one indiscretion.

My most devastating unfaithful act was betraying not only Jackson but also the woman who was my best friend at the time. Yes, I was *that* woman. The woman who is seen as the ultimate guilty seducer—the one who is fully responsible for the act. And truth be told, my behavior deserved to be judged accordingly, even though I was not the only guilty party.

I had responded to my best friend's husband's interest in me. I was interested; he flirted with me. I flirted back; he emotionally encouraged me. I encouraged him, and over time, I fell into the delusional fantasy that attraction and seduction somehow would offer me something I had never experienced before and was unlikely to experience ever again.

My moral compass spun out of control, jarred by a magnetic moment.

Obviously, the electrical current that jarred my moral compass was the connection between the needs of this man who was looking for something he thought was missing within himself and my own need to find what I thought was missing within me. My due north was no longer pointing in the right direction.

The added strong current—which I had not yet discovered—was my past trauma and its hidden messages that unconsciously dictated my actions and behavior.

The ripple effect of this affair was soon felt. News spread quickly to most everyone we knew. I went numb, unable to completely grasp the magnitude of what had happened. I reverted to my inner mode of surviving by numbing myself.

Dissociation had become a way for me to escape internally when a literal escape was not available to me.[3]

At the time of the affair, it would still be another two years until my past would erupt before my eyes, forcing me to face what I had repressed all my life. Unbeknownst to me, being exposed by this affair peeled back a heavy layer of hiddenness that I had developed as a child to survive.

I took full responsibility for my behavior. I took the blame, as well I should have.

I have shared the following thoughts with many survivors of trauma who have had an affair or were considering having an affair. I wish someone would have said these things to me at the time:

> Whatever behaviors you have done that have hurt you and others, take responsibility.
>
> There is a reason why you made the decisions that you did, and these reasons need to be discovered, healed, and overcome.

---

[3] "Dissociation is the essence of trauma. The overwhelming experience is split off and fragmented, so that the emotions, sounds, images, thoughts, and physical sensations related to the trauma take on a life of their own. The sensory fragments of memory intrude into the present, where they are literally relived." Bessel van der Kolk, *The Body Keeps the Score: Brain, Mind, and Body in the Healing of Trauma* (New York: Penguin Books, 2014), 66.

There is an explanation for what happened and why you did what you did, but the explanation does not justify your behavior—it only explains it.

Therefore, it is necessary to face and own whatever has happened by taking responsibility for your actions and doing whatever you can and is necessary to clean up the aftermath. But at the same time, always hold this truth close to you: your behaviors cannot define your true self.

Reckless decisions that induced pain will—for a time—obscure your ability to see yourself for who you truly are. But here is the truth. Whatever you may have done, your actions cannot ultimately define you, unless you choose to ignore what has happened and do nothing about it.

At the time of my transgression, I did take responsibility. I invited my friend—who was understandably now my ex-friend—into a meeting with a mediator. I owned all that I had done and apologized. She vented and raged, which she had every right to do. I listened, and when she left, I never saw her again.

Forty years later, I did find out that she and her family had moved to another state. She and her husband are still together, for which I am grateful.

After that conversation, an onslaught of days of overwhelming drama unfolded. A couple of weeks later, the initial shock began to wear off. I began to feel myself pulled into a pit of guilt, shame, despair, and depression. I found myself becoming less able to function. Within a few short weeks, the therapist I was seeing at the time thought I needed additional help.

I entered a treatment center for two weeks. At first this felt like an added trauma, but it soon became a safe place for me to process and sort out what I had done and what I needed to do next.

It was while I was in treatment that I knew I needed to divorce Jackson. This was a painful, complicated, and agonizing decision for me to make. Morally, I hated the thought of divorce. I wrestled openly and honestly with what I grew up believing, that divorce was unthinkable—and two divorces were *definitely* unthinkable. But I knew if I was to face whatever was going on inside me, I could not do it while married to Jackson. There was too much damage, and our two years in couples therapy had not made a difference for either of us.

My decision to divorce Jackson gave him a legitimate reason for the divorce, allowing him to move on with his life. Divorcing gave me an opportunity to dive deeper into my own recovery, hopefully to find out what on earth was going on with me.

Did I feel remorse? Lordy, did I ever feel remorse. The bomb that I set off impacted Jackson, my children, my friends, my community that had previously respected me, and, of course, myself. I watched as the damage that I had done and the pain that I felt bored deeper into my soul. I knew that my apologies offered no real healing, but I offered them anyway, in the hope that one day they might hold some value in the lives of those I had so deeply wounded and betrayed.

I saw the pain on my daughters' faces when Jackson and I told them we were divorcing. I heard their cries and the anger from one of my daughters when she said, "You promised you would *never* divorce again!" It did not matter that there were many reasons for my decision to divorce. I was the one causing all this pain in my precious daughters' lives, and my heart was breaking. Yes, I was filled with agonizing remorse.

Even though I have owned the pain and suffering I caused my daughters and I have forgiven myself, it lingers, because what they went through is something I cannot imagine ever having done to my girls, whom I so dearly love.

I cried out to God for forgiveness, and I knew I had it, but it would take me far longer to forgive myself.

There were people who would not forgive me, who outwardly judged me harshly for what I had done. It was not for me to judge them or their reasons for their condemnation. I would have to decide how I would best deal with their judgments. I needed to learn how to honor their feelings—which I did, but it was difficult to do. I had to feel the pain of remorse even in the most difficult of encounters I would face. In each case, I was being given the opportunity to resist rising to my defense, to listen humbly, and to honor how others had been impacted by my choices. This was key in developing a new course for my life.

For many months, I had regrets and doubts about my decision to divorce, wondering if it was the right thing to do—while at the same time knowing I had made the right decision.

I stayed the course as I rode an emotional roller coaster of ups and downs for more than a year until the divorce became final.

I had a great deal of healing to do around the current trauma that I had created for myself when I entered the affair. I needed to keep my head above the drowning line; I needed to face honestly this twisted event in my life; I needed to sort out my feelings from my thinking and from reality. I needed this time in my life where I could focus on myself, my healing, and my regrets.

I eventually discovered that the ill purpose of regret was to tether me to the past and to torment me with everything I had ever done wrong.

Regret was meant to be a temporary step, a layover, as I moved toward freedom in my life. It was not meant to be a permanent destination.

Feeling regret is a spotlight that *something* needs to be dealt with, but it should not redefine me as a person.

Regret is meant to be a momentary revelation to see that I could have done things differently, if only I had made a different choice. It was then that regret became my teacher, having served its sole purpose in my life.

I recently came across this quote by embodied healing coach Syanna Wand, which so eloquently says what I came to discover so many years ago in my healing journey:

How to hold regret tenderly:
I wish I would have done that differently;
and,
at the time, I couldn't.

Reflection on My Story

Jackson: He remarried a wonderful woman who is a beautiful fit for his life. They have been happily married and share a fulfilling life together. Jackson has been a caring and good father to our three girls and now to our grandchildren. One of the kind exchanges that I have with Jackson is when we meet for a family wedding, grandchild event, or other celebration. Jackson always greets me with, "Hello, friend." This is evidence of forgiveness.

My daughters: I have a loving and close relationship with each of my three girls. The ultimate blessing I received in being married to Jackson was having two additional daughters. They are amazing wives and mothers who have, among the three of them, raised eight incredible children.

It has taken time for them to work through the difficulty of having a mom who needed as much recovery as I required, but I was determined that the gift I would give them was the promise that, no matter how unraveled a shape I was in, I was not going to leave them with this memory of me. I would overcome and become the woman and the mother they so deserved to have. I did my healing for myself, but I also did it because I wanted to be a mom they would be proud of for doing whatever it took to become the person I was meant to be and the mom and grandmother that I could become.

So many years have passed since these events occurred in my story. The beauty of new life exists. One thing I have learned is that time, healing, and growth have the power to redirect our paths. I have always had a choice, but I had to deal with what was keeping me from being able to make choices that would benefit me, instead causing me to make choices that would harm me.

I remember speaking to a minister after I had made numerous changes in my life and was wondering why I still had so much crap to deal with. He said something to me that I will never forget.

"You sowed a lot of negative seeds in your young adult life, and this is what has grown up as weeds and must be harvested and thrown away. Over the last years, you have sown good seed, but it has not yet become the predominant crop to choke out the weeds. But because you are no longer sowing negative seeds, the good seed will eventually eliminate all negative growth. Give it time. You will see some great harvests in your life that will wipe out all evidence of what was once there."

He was right. For decades, I have been harvesting beautiful, rich, fulfilling harvests. Transformation is possible—with dedication, healing, and time.

The Betrayer

Further Reflection on My Story

When fear is the predominant influence on my thinking (even my well-meaning intentions), it can cause me to miss the mark. Such was the case in writing this chapter, "The Betrayer." I missed the obvious mark that I did not and could not see until after the fact. Here is my current-day story.

I had worried many months about writing my next chapter, "The Betrayer." The empty white page continued to stare me in the face. *Where do I begin? How do I say what needs to be said? Is it too high a risk to expose myself in this way?*

I felt the strong current of fear pulling me away from writing. Inside my head I heard, *Just skip this chapter and move on. No real need to do this to yourself.* I found myself agreeing with this thought that sounded so reasonable. Yet I knew if I was to be open and honest, I must write this chapter acknowledging that I, too, was a betrayer. How would it be right for me to share this chapter, "Betrayed," without honestly owning how I had been a betrayer?

As I began to allow the words to fall upon the page, I felt again the waves of shame and regret that were wrapped around each experience. Fear increased as my imagination reminded me of the scenarios I had seen play out in my mind. Every scenario ended with one, or all three, of my daughters rejecting me in some way. *I cannot bear the thought of this.*

The wrestling continued. *Do I just send them this chapter? Do I send the entire manuscript? There is no good way to handle this.* Over many weeks, I continued to process the best way to let my daughters into this time in my life. I felt my fear rise and shed tears over how I have hurt them—and how this part of my story may wound them once again.

I finally concluded that if they could read the entirety of my manuscript, then perhaps the chapter on being the betrayer would make more sense to them. *Surely this must be the best way for them to read this truth I have withheld from them.* Making this decision, I found a sense of relief in completing this chapter, "The Betrayer."

The day came when the manuscript was complete—or so I thought. I sent it to them and felt a sense of relief that they would now have the truth that I had withheld from them. What I did not realize was that fear was directing this decision. The thought of one of my daughters rejecting me was far too great for me to face. This fear influenced my decision to send them the manuscript, rather than speak to them directly.

It was not until after one of my daughters read the manuscript that what should have been obvious to me came into focus. She let me know what my fear had not allowed me to see: that a personal conversation with all three of my daughters would have been the better choice. I missed it. I missed the mark to their hearts.

I could see how my decision to have them read the manuscript, rather than speak to them directly, made it about me. I had wanted them to better understand *me* in terms of how I came to make destructive choices in my life.

But as their mom, I needed to make revealing my past in "The Betrayer" about *them*.

How could I have missed something that I knew to do and that was so blatantly obvious?

Fear. Fear had that kind of power over me, erasing the most relational option I could have chosen.

This is my problem to deal with and to correct with my daughters. This I am doing. I have again learned something about myself that I needed to see. I also needed to tell you, my readers, so that you can understand the power that fear can have over us, knowingly or unknowingly, when we have hidden shame.

The good news is this: fear just lost another hold on me, because I know how much I love my daughters and how much they love me. Being honest with them cannot change this.

What Is Your Story?

Have you ever entered a situation that you later regretted?

How did you handle it? Did you face it head-on, avoid it entirely, or deny it by saying it didn't matter? Did you minimize the situation or blame someone else for what happened?

How did the experience impact your life emotionally, mentally, and physically?

Did you have feelings of guilt, shame, humiliation, or failure? How did you work through these feelings?

Share Your Story

If ever there was a time to share your story, it is when you'd prefer it to remain hidden. Hiding the truth will hold you captive to secrecy, and secrecy will guide you into cover-ups and lies. This never ends well.

What is the worst thing that could happen if you shared your story? List all the fears and concerns that you have about sharing your story. If you still feel like you are unable to be open with your story, a good place to start is to journal or write about it—for your eyes only.

When you feel ready, now share your story with someone you trust. If you need absolute assurance of confidentiality, share it with a professional who is a good fit for you. What is important is to offer your story to someone who will hold it with compassion and understanding, because you deserve this.

9

Early Morning Dip

I lie motionless in my bunk, not wanting to disturb the nine other slumbering campers still wrapped tight in their sleeping bags. Far in the distance, the bell that woke me continues to ring, announcing to all brave campers that in thirty minutes, the early-morning dip will begin.

Three mornings have passed, and on each I have been determined to be the first camper ready to dive into the lake at five-thirty a.m. Yet with each passing five a.m. bell, I have talked myself out of it. Five o'clock is way too early to awaken into the muted northern light of summer. The cabin is chilled, and the warmth of my nest whispers, "Don't leave." Knowing I only have two more days before I must return home, however, I decide that today is the day. It's now or never.

Come on, just go for it! With that internal proclamation, I toss aside the blanket atop my bag. Ever so quietly, I maneuver myself out of the Air Force sleeping bag that my brother has given to our family. Exiting the cocoon of warmth created throughout the night, I suddenly feel I've made a big mistake. Yet despite my inner debate, determination wins out.

As I quietly inch myself down from my top bunk, I am hit with the chill of our unheated cabin. The shock obliterates all sleepiness. *Dang, this cabin is freezing! What am I thinking?*

Okay, Step One complete. I mentally check "Get out of bed" off my list. I encourage myself to keep going—no turning back.

I remove my pajamas and step into my freezing-cold bathing suit, which has refused to dry from yesterday's afternoon swim. This predicted torture causes me to pause, but if I want to reach my goal, I have to put on this iceberg I now hold in my hand. I affirm to myself one last time, *No turning back!*

Pulling on the paisley pink-and-blue suit, the penetrating cold clings to my skin, sending painful shock waves through my body. I gasp, trying my best not to cry aloud and wake everyone in the cabin. Biting my tongue, I slip my arms through the straps and grab my damp swim towel, wrapping it around my shoulders. There is no warmth to be had from my thinning, moist towel, but strangely enough I believe this cover offers me a modicum of relief from the elements I have chosen to face.

Slipping on my sandals, I quietly open the cabin door, closing it gently behind me, and begin my trek down the path to the lake.

Big Sandy Lake in northern Minnesota has become a haven I look forward to every summer—my escape where,

Early Morning Dip

for one week, I find the freedom to be myself. This particular year, I have turned fourteen just one month before camp. Being in junior high allows me to enjoy newfound freedoms, this morning being one of the perks allowed to a junior-higher. I am old enough for a morning dip—shivers and all.

As I venture onto the well-worn path that finds its way through the pine-filled forest, I pause to watch a canopy of fog dance through the trees. It creates an enveloping stillness that wraps itself around me. The pines, bathed in yesterday's evening rain, press their fresh scent into my nostrils. In the distance, the intermittent call of loons on the lake carries up the path.

I continue my descent down the hill, pausing as the lake comes into view through the predawn light. Before me is a vast expanse of the lake, bordered with shoreline hardwoods combined with white and red pine. On the surface, steaming clouds of vapor float upward—a result of the water being warmer than the surrounding air.

The call of the loons grows louder as I make my way to the shore. Their haunting cries carry from all directions over the many acres of lake surface. This same ominous, mystical, and ancient sound woos me as I fall asleep and generates a hypnotic curiosity during the day as I watch them bob up and down upon the waves. The calls seem to transcend time from before human existence. In this moment, I have been invited to a private concert of the loons.

The lifeguards arrive, taking their position in their white tower. Other campers appear, some eagerly pushing the boundary of the water's edge with their toes, knowing that there is no entry into the lake until the whistle blows. As the minutes tick by, more campers arrive, all shivering in the chill of the morning air. As cold as I have become, I wonder how I will ever be able to enter the water. My body shaking nearly uncontrollably, I wonder if this will be worth it.

The countdown begins. Towels fall from early-teen bodies onto the sand. A blasting whistle cuts the air, and delighted squeals of eager swimmers fill the early morning as they plunge into the open-mouthed lake before them. I soon follow, more hesitant. Placing my foot in the water, I am taken aback that it feels like a lukewarm bath. I realize that by running in, I will soon warm my chilled-to-the-bone body.

Discarding all hesitation, I run as fast as I can into the dark liquid until the water rises to my chest, keeping me from being able to feel the sand, except by brief toe touches.

It is time. I plunge forward, spreading my arms out in front of me in rhythmic strokes. I move past other swimmers, motivated now to swim farther out to the ropes and floating wooden dock. There are only two other swimmers who have ventured out this far, and I am determined to be the third.

I move away from the pair, who find their way onto the dock to dive. I have no desire to follow in their games of who can dive deeper or chase the farthest after a ball. Something inside me looks to distance myself. I want to experience a restful back float, claiming a section of the lake as my own.

Early Morning Dip

Finding my spot within the boundary of the ropes, I give myself permission to let go. As I lie back on the bed of liquid, my arms move gently, keeping me afloat. My ears, resting beneath the surface, silence the world around me, and I enter into an experience that I had not known exists.

I am cradled and gently rocked by the soft ripple of waves. I begin to feel that I am one with the lake, sandwiched between the warmth beneath me and the coolness that breathes over me. I am embraced by the water, floating on a surface of luxuriant silk.

My eyes gaze at the thin line of early light attempting to part the last elements of darkness from the sky above me. Low-hanging, heavy clouds linger from the rainstorm the night before, leaving an ominous light caught between night and day. I lift my head slightly above the water's surface to hear the echoing call of loons in full chorus. I do not understand what I am experiencing, but something deep inside me is awakening to a reality that is foreign to me.

I am one with the lake—the loons, the dawn, the end of night—one with myself and something greater than myself.

Unaware, I am oblivious to the existence of time.

But the advancing light rising from the horizon's entrance pulls me back to the present. . . to consciousness. I have been carried into a new day.

The blowing whistles screech as everyone is called out of the lake. Swimmers are to return to their cabins to find their way to the showers. Within the hour, all campers will be in the dining hall, eating a delicious breakfast, singing songs, finding reasons to laugh hysterically. The day will unfold with games, contests, archery, and even marksmanship—which I will ace, beating even the best that the boys can show—though I have never shot a rifle before.

There will be two chapel services, one at ten a.m. and one at seven p.m. There will be a sing-along and a message about Jesus and His love for all of us and why it is important that we not do bad things. I have heard it all before, and I will show interest, but my mind will wander back to what I experienced earlier that morning—this moment that lures me to its memory.

I have entered the early morning dip and discovered oneness with life. Alone in a newfound reality within the lake, I have had a baptism of sorts that transcends my religious understanding. I am one with creation, with God, and I know for the first time in my fourteen years of life that I exist. That I belong. That I am a part of everything that surrounds me.

On this morning many years ago, the seed of being loved, known, and valued found its way into the deepest part of my being. Over the years, that seed has continued to grow. To this day, it lives on to reveal a deeper truth of who I am and who I am becoming.

Reflection on My Story

At the age of fourteen, I did not have the capacity to hold wisdom, nor a deeper understanding of this experience that gifted me with awareness and meaning. My lack of understanding, however, did not deprive me of such an experience. Since my early-morning dip, I have been blessed many times over with a variety of greater-than-myself encounters. They exist. I didn't go searching for them—they came to me as a gift to embrace, to enjoy, and most importantly to guide me, teach me, and even heal areas in my life that I did not realize needed healing. Each experience has given me the opportunity to discover life's meaning, purpose, and wisdom.

These moments also reveal the blessing in all of my circumstances, no matter how hidden these blessings are in the moment. Each holds a gemstone of wisdom, growth, and truth. They are personal treasures from which I glean value.

Even though many years have passed since this morning-dip experience, this memory still holds treasures that I am only now able to see and understand. There are deeper insights for me to discover, even from my past experiences. I suspect treasures such as these remain eternal.

What Is Your Story?

Consider taking time for personal reflection on your own story.

What are the experiences you have had that have affected your life? A moment, an event, or an experience that offered something of greater meaning and value in your life?

How were you inspired or encouraged?

How did the experience awaken a deeper understanding of truth and purpose for you?

Share Your Story

When you give voice to your experience, you will discover more about yourself and others and how you are woven into the fabric of this life. In sharing your story, you offer hope, wisdom, and love to the one who will listen and receive your gift.

Be discerning. Your intuition and heart will guide you to the person or people with whom you can safely share your story. If by chance you share and that person does not listen, move on, knowing that your sharing is not lost or wasted. You will learn and discover great things from this experience, as well as having placed the seed of truth into someone who needs it.

10

Hit from All Sides

"Class, settle down!" Mrs. Sneed's voice was directive and loud enough to make herself heard above her classroom full of third graders returning from lunch and recess.

"Take your seats quickly now, and take out your arithmetic books," she continued. "Today we are going to use the blackboard, and I will have some of you come up to do problems on the board."

The cold familiar feeling of fear began to run through my body as I found my desk and quickly sat down. I hated the blackboard and the feeling of impending doom that arose from the thought of being asked to answer problems before the whole class. I hated numbers but loved letters. I did not want my teacher to call on me and did my best to disappear from her sight.

I began to shrink down into my chair to hide behind my desk, in the hope of making myself invisible.

Mrs. Sneed said, "Jimmy and Mary, please come up to the blackboard." Jimmy and Mary quickly popped out of their desks as a wave of relief flowed over my body. They drew the number configurations on the board, wrote their answers beneath the line, and received Mrs. Sneed's approval. "Correct! You may go back to your desks."

Another two children were called up to the board, and again I was passed by without notice. I began to feel safe that I would not be chosen to face the wretched blackboard.

As the last two students turned to find their way back to their desks, Mrs. Sneed announced, "Tommy and Faith, please come to the blackboard."

I felt my breath catch in my throat, and my legs began to freeze. I did not want to go up there, but obedience was required. Slowly, I turned my legs to exit my desk chair. Tommy was already halfway to the board as I took my first step toward the flat black monolith before me.

Everything inside me began to shut down. My attention was focused on moving my legs. I could no longer hear what was happening in the room. Terror was quickly overtaking me. As I reached the blackboard, all my motions slowed. I watched as my hand reached for a piece of chalk on the thin metal shelf attached to the board's bottom edge.

Tommy had already completed his numeric task and was returning to his desk. All alone at the blackboard, I began to write the first numbers on the board as Mrs. Sneed dictated.

After the problem was displayed for the class to see, I felt my arm come down to my side, clutching the white chunk in my hand. I stared at the figures I had just drawn, but all was blurred and distorted. I was frozen.

From somewhere in the distance I heard, "Faith, answer the problem." It was Mrs. Sneed's voice, but I could not move to turn toward her. My eyes were locked on the white fuzzy mass on the background of black that held me captive.

A second time, I heard her voice, "Faith, answer the problem." Her voice now sounded like it was coming from farther away than it had just moments before. Had she moved, or was I fading?

I stood motionless, not knowing what to do until I heard Mrs. Sneed's voice carry a harsh edge, replacing her usual kind tone. Was it frustration or agitation I heard? Was I in trouble? Would I be punished? "Go back to your seat. Go sit down!"

I felt my small hand place the chalk back onto the silver tray filled with various sizes of chalk and erasers. I turned slowly, knowing that every eye in the class would be watching me take the long journey back to my desk. I lowered my head. Shame had overcome any sense of myself, of my existence. I wanted to cry, but dared not.

Was it a few weeks or months before I heard Mrs. Sneed's next request of me? I don't always remember the sequence of events clearly, but the incidents themselves are embedded into my memory.

"Faith, would you come to my desk, please?"

Every head in my third grade class turned toward me. The sound of my teacher's voice gave no sign as to why she would be calling me to her desk. I slowly moved my legs out from under my desktop and did as I was told.

When I reached her desk, all eyes were on me and our teacher. Mrs. Sneed pulled me to her side and in a lower voice asked, "Faith, where is your paper that was to be turned in today?"

I answered, "I put it on your desk; I don't know where it is." I knew I was lying, but I was so terrified of what she might do to me, I just couldn't tell the truth.

She continued, "Faith, I have been through all the papers on my desk, and your paper is not here. Did you leave it at home? Did you not do the homework?"

Again I said, "I *did* put it on your desk."

I had been taught never to lie, and with each lie, the weight of guilt grew heavier. I rarely lied, because keeping the rules was imperative if I was to feel safe from being called a "naughty" girl—which later, with age, would become the sinful woman that I heard my mom and other women talk about. I had to keep the rules so as not to be found naughty or sinful.

Mrs. Sneed was insistent that I had not turned in my paper, but I held to my lie.

She told me to go back to my desk, and I obeyed. The recess time was about to begin, which meant we would all go down to the lunchroom to get our glass of milk from the large silver machine. Each of us hoped we would be the person, if the milk dispenser ran out of milk, who would claim the white marble that would appear when it ran empty, making the marble proudly ours to own. It was a childhood lottery game that was rarely won.

After our glass of milk, the playground waited for us with swings, slides, and merry-go-rounds.

Mrs. Sneed must have known that I was lying. I felt the weight of that unspoken judgment as if I would always carry it. Yet I knew I had to bear it because I *was* guilty. I just could not handle seeing my classmates again. I had to find a way to escape the guilt that was painfully squeezing the air from my chest.

I went into the cloak room, where all our jackets were hung neatly under our names. One by one, my classmates grabbed their jackets and ran out the door to line up for morning break time. I lingered, hiding behind my coat. When the cloakroom was empty, I quickly grabbed my coat, ran down the stairs and out the front door—not the door onto the playground.

Escaping, I headed for my house. When I arrived, my mother said, "What are you doing home?"

"I'm sick, Mom. I don't feel good," I replied.

She did the mothering "check out" of what it might be, then told me to go and climb into bed. I did as I was told.

As I lay there in my bed, I felt a huge sense of relief. I was safe in my bed, away from Mrs. Sneed and my lie. I somehow began to believe that I would never be found out.

Sometime later, my mother and father both opened the door to my room. Mom did the speaking. "Faith, the principal just called the house. She was wondering if you were here at home. When I told her you were, she explained that the school did not know where you had gone. You just left school without telling anyone?"

"Yes, I left school."

My mother's voice became suddenly angry, harsh, and blaming. "We don't have time for this! We have enough happening with your brother right now. We don't need this aggravation and you adding to what we are dealing with. You stay in bed for the rest of the day!"

She and my dad—who did not say one word about what I had done—turned, closed the door, and walked away.

I was now totally alone. No one had asked what was going on or why I did what I did. In fact, it was never spoken of again.

I was left to store within myself the judgment that had been placed on me by Mrs. Sneed, my parents, and myself. I *was* the naughty girl.

～

I never knew that I had to deal with things that happened to me in life, because I had been shown by my parents' actions that you either ignored things or you prayed that they would go away. It would be many more years before I discovered that you could actually resolve issues in life— even things that had happened many years ago. So, my time in Mrs. Sneed's classroom went onto a shelf deep within my subconscious as a child—but the impact of that day carried into my future.

As time marched on, I entered into my twenties, and there was only one decent place to go for fun in the small town I currently lived in: the Holiday Inn.

On one particular evening I had dinner, then decided to stay for a while to listen to the country band that had been hired for the week. I ordered a drink and let the week's demands fall away.

People were dancing, which was, and continues to be, one of my favorite people-watching events.

A nice-looking cowboy came over and asked if I would like to dance. I told him I was not a great dancer because I had never been taught how. He responded, "No problem."

I went on the dance floor with him, and we began to dance. It hadn't been more than a couple of minutes of dancing before he loudly and emphatically said, "You dance like a fish!" He walked away, leaving me on the floor alone, with other dancers staring at me.

Rejected!

Thirty some years later, I was asked to oversee and lead a committee I was interested in. I accepted.

There was a woman on the committee who was not pleased with this decision. It could have been jealousy, believing that she would have been the better choice for my position. I don't know what motivated her feelings toward me, but she did not hold back in expressing them.

My response to her and the committee was to listen intently, confirm their ideas, and show patience and respect.

At our first meeting, she challenged some of the materials I had previously sent out to each member. It felt like nitpicking, but I listened to her concerns. The following week I received a confrontational email from her telling me all the various ways I had missed the mark, which in her opinion gave her the right to judge how my leadership needed improvement.

I made a point of responding kindly, hearing her concerns, and offering my goals and vision in overseeing the future of the committee.

She still had more to say about how I was inadequate as a leader and a person. I felt minimized, not seen, not valued. In a word, dismissed.

Why would this ridiculous encounter leave me feeling this way? I wondered. *Surely there must be something unresolved within her. Or is there something unresolved within me or both of us?* I needed to sort this out.

It took a few days to conclude that she had hit a vulnerable area, one to which I found it difficult not to react. Feeling misjudged or believing that my character is being redefined by someone was a trap that caused a negative reaction in me, and I ended up overreacting.

I had worked hard to become the person I felt at peace with. I wanted to be seen for who I had become. When that didn't happen, this was my problem to deal with, not hers.

My inability to leave her words on her side of the court exposed an area within me that needed attention. The kindness and respect I offered her was rejected. It all tied back to encounters with my childhood abusers as well as cruel high school bullies who had humiliated me. Now I was triggered by someone I met in a committee meeting who, from my past experiences, I perceived to be a bully.

Author's Comment: *This next story occurred in a religious setting. In sharing my story, I am in no way saying that there is a particular religion or denomination that is better or more damaging than another. There are honorable followers within the congregations of all religious beliefs, and there are those who have a far more controlling, legalistic approach with their congregants. Any time a person is made to fall under the control of another—or face persecution if they do not—this creates an experience harmful to one's soul and spirit.*

Definition of persecution, *according to Dictionary.com: "To pursue with harassing or oppressive treatment, especially because of religious or political beliefs, ethnic or racial origin, gender identity, or sexual orientation."*

I was excited to join a new congregation that was forming because it was to be a smaller church community. I had come to know the minister and his family, and their vision for this church aligned with my own: connecting and healing hearts by offering mercy, compassion, and encouragement to each other.

Those who decided to be a part of this new adventure were all fun-loving people, and our excitement grew as we found a place in which to worship together. Once we were up and going, it wasn't long before our congregation grew in numbers. We made friends, gathered socially, and were proactive in serving each other when needs arose. I enjoyed being able to help: singing in groups, planning retreats, caring for others' needs.

Over the next few years, I was encouraged to consider being on the elder board. This was a group of members who oversaw the running of the church, helped to resolve issues that arose, and made sure the needs of the congregation were met. I was eager to serve and found it to be a good niche for me.

That is, until a certain couple came into our church. In the beginning, they were a delight to get to know and soon became engaged in many of the areas. I sensed that something was not all aboveboard, as I felt a bit of hesitancy with them, but dismissed my feeling as being too cautious. I didn't want to be quick to make assumptions.

In the months that followed, Mr. and Mrs. Sheridan began to integrate themselves into the lives of the leaders and select members of this church. This, in and of itself, was not a problem. The problem was that secrets seemed to be forming. Chosen members were invited to special get-togethers, while others were excluded. Some people began to raise concerns and question the behavior of certain congregants—something which had not been the norm before this point.

For example, one woman in the church had suddenly lost her forty-year-old husband to an aneurysm. The way she chose to grieve on the day he died was scrutinized, criticized, and even judged as unholy. I stood up for this grieving widow. Some accepted my argument on her behalf, and others did not.

In the months to come, several of the congregants, led by Mr. and Mrs. Sheridan, began taking other congregants out of town to hear teaching in a city an hour away. Sometimes it would be for an evening meeting; other times it would be for a week's worth of meetings. Our pastor and his family also joined in on some of these meetings.

I was never invited to go, probably because they knew I wouldn't go if asked. They most likely had observed various members coming to me with their concerns. I was outspoken and clear in my opinion that the church was not meant to be a place for gossip, hurting others, or creating dissension.

As the months passed, there were more murmurings as subtle pieces of gossip began to circulate. People were being hurt as damaging assumptions were made about them. Multiple people came to me to share their wounded hearts. What had been a peaceful, safe, and loving community was now falling apart.

Mrs. Sheridan rose into a more authoritative position as she was perceived as "knowing" something spiritually that no one else knew about. In many people's eyes, she was leading them to a deeper truth by taking them to these meetings an hour away.

Then came the Sunday when it was announced that, on a particular Saturday coming up, a special speaker was coming to the church to teach the church how to speak in tongues or, as it is also called, the use of *glossolalia*. This is considered a spiritual language that is not understandable unless someone is divinely inspired to interpret it.

Red flags went up inside me. I am not opposed to anyone speaking in tongues, and I know that many believers in Christianity, as well as in other faiths and beliefs, use this form of deeper connection and meditation according to their convictions.

On that Saturday, I sat to listen to what this speaker had to say. As she spoke, I became more concerned. Her teaching was absolute—she left no room for anyone *not* to speak in tongues.

As her teaching ended, she began to tell the attendees what to do to begin to speak in tongues.

At this point, my concern multiplied. To be told that there was a higher level of spirituality if someone spoke in tongues placed judgment on everyone who did not do this.

Church members began coming over to me in tears, unable to do what this teacher was teaching. They had tried and failed and tried and failed, and now felt like something was wrong with them for not being able to speak in tongues. I put my arm around each. "There is nothing wrong with you," I said. "You are a gifted person with so much to offer. Do not believe the lie that you are the problem. You are not the problem." My heart broke for these dear people who felt like failures because they couldn't do what was expected of them.

At the next elder board meeting, I made no bones about it that what had happened was not okay. People were hurting because they were not able to make something happen that was not actually required for them to make happen. Yet they had been made to feel it was a requirement. I took a stand for the hearts of the men and women who were hurting, which I believed was more important than emphasizing speaking in tongues. For all people there should be increased joy, encouragement, and purpose in coming together, not less.

My stand began what became many months of being accused of not following the leadership of the church. I don't remember how many endless meetings I had with the pastor, other elders, and other members. With each one, I would leave feeling that things were resolved, only to find out later that things were worse behind the scenes. A few people backed me up, but most began to withdraw from me.

My husband left the church before I did. He had had enough and was concerned for me. I thought I could see it through, but within a few months, the final blow came. A meeting of the elders was scheduled, and I was told I needed to attend. (I was no longer on the elder board by this time.)

The date and time were set. My husband was unavailable, so I would be going alone. When my daughter heard this, she and her husband said they would come with me.

When we arrived, there were several cars already parked nearby. I thought little of it in the moment, but when I entered the home where the meeting was to be held, I saw not only the elder board but also all of their wives in attendance, along with Mr. and Mrs. Sheridan and a few others who I would soon learn were my accusers. Everyone was already seated when we arrived.

Someone showed me where to sit with my daughter and son-in-law. The room was filled with people I knew, some of them close friends with whom I had shared my life, even some of my painful experiences. The meeting came to order.

The pastor spoke for a few minutes, then stood and laid out the rules of the evening. 1) I was not to speak at any time during the meeting. 2) I was only to listen. 3) At the end, I would be told what I was to do.

I was now numb and in shock. I found myself repressing a pain that wanted to erupt from deep within. My mind raced with wonderful memories of what we had originally formed together, comparing it with the now-oppressive atmosphere hanging over the room. It felt dark and ominous. I wanted to run, and yet I wanted to hear what I was being accused of.

The tribunal began.

The order of things is inconsequential, and I do not remember anyway. What I do remember is that I was accused of disobedience, of hurting or harming Mrs. Sheridan, of wounding someone else for a reason I do not recall. Mostly, I was accused of causing dissension by standing up for the people who had been wounded. I know there were other things that were said that evening, but since I had no recourse, I must have placed it all in the "it-doesn't-matter-anyway" file. I was not allowed to speak to defend myself, so what did it matter?

Hit from All Sides

When all of their accusations had been spoken against me, I was told what I would need to do. For one year, I was not to have any say within the church; I was to be silent. I was to go to the location an hour away where all the teaching was happening and be under their authority until I was restored back into community—which would be within the year.

I did not hear another word after this. A voice of strength, love, and truth rose up within me. *"The ties are cut! You are free to leave. Do not stay any longer."*

I caught my breath as I felt a weight lift off me. I had tears in my eyes at the same time from the pain that had just been inflicted on me, but I knew I was now free.

The meeting ended. Many could not look me in the face, though some showed a few droplets of compassion. Mrs. Sheridan stood, very pleased at the results of the meeting. When I got to my son-in-law's car, I burst into tears from the trauma I had been through over the past several months. I felt relief to be out of there, combined with the sorrow of losing so many I had considered dear friends.

I had just felt the sting of being persecuted by spiritual abuse. At the same time, I was set free to begin a journey that would take me beyond the lies and accusations of that evening.

I had always feared being persecuted, but in time (after processing what had happened to me), I would find that my identity—my true self—had been strengthened because of it. I not only survived, I healed and began thriving.

Treasure Found

Reflection on My Story

It is likely all of us will experience shame, judgment, rejection, and even persecution at some point. Our definitions of these mistreatments will vary. Whether we believe another's experience fits our concept or not, it is of key importance to value another person's experience and the story behind it with compassion, or we risk becoming the shamer, the judge, the rejecter, or even the persecutor.

As I reflect back on each of these stories, I realize how far I have come. There were years that I was filled with anger at what I experienced as a child and as an adult. There were months of sadness, blaming myself, not understanding why my heart was so vulnerable and sensitive. Eventually, I came to the place where I could forgive and release each and every person who had wounded me. Yes, even Mrs. Sheridan—who took me the longest to fully forgive. Ultimately, forgiving was the only way for me to completely heal the gashes that had been thrust into my psyche.

The takeaway is that I *did* heal. I overcame. I refused to be a victim to another person who wanted to have power over me. I opened myself up to learn from past experiences, rather than ignore or run from them. They became my teacher over many years as I asked myself questions: *What could I have done differently? Why was I unable to speak up? What would it sound like for me to say "No!" or "Stop!" or just turn and walk away?*

Lastly, and I admittedly own this, there are times when it is still hard for me to ignore the lies and rejection that come with false judgments. I use my skills to walk through these encounters, but it can pack a hard punch to my heart. Healing is an ongoing journey, but I cannot imagine ever leaving the journey to peace and freedom.

What Is Your Story?

How have you experienced judgment or being shamed, rejected, or persecuted in your life?

Did you ignore what happened to you? Did you minimize the event? What did you do with what happened to you?

Have you considered how these occurrences may have had a long-term impact on your current everyday life?

Share Your Story

If you have never shared your experiences with someone, you might consider the reasons as to why you have chosen not to share your story.

Your stories matter, because *you* matter. Giving voice to your story validates you—and confirms that what happened to you was unacceptable.

What happened to you may appear insignificant, but it wasn't. Acknowledging that these events in your life were wrong and that any mistreatment you received was not your fault will likely bring immeasurable freedom and closure in your life.

A helpful measuring stick to see if these incidents were inconsequential is to ask yourself these two questions:

If I think about what happened to me, do I feel anger, resentment, or even vengeance—wanting them to pay for what they did to me?

Or...

Can I honestly forgive the person or people who hurt me?

If you answered yes to the first question—share your story with someone who can support you, hear you, and encourage you.

If you answered yes to the second question, share your story with someone who has not yet been able to forgive. Having been there gives rise to empathy that then becomes an integral part of healing in another person's life.

Forgiveness, by the way, is not a one-and-done either. Forgiveness is a process that you choose to invest in. Sometimes we can forgive quickly; other times it takes time. If you want to get to the place where you can forgive, then choose to do so. It doesn't mean that you will be able to forgive immediately, but you can always continue to move toward that day by your choice. Be honest with yourself and stay the course. The day will come when you can liberate yourself from the heavy feelings you feel toward another.

Remember, sharing your story with a confidant is a key piece in healing an old wound. If you do not have someone you believe you can trust, turn to a professional who will hold your story in confidence and will walk you through what may be holding you back.

11

The Destroyer, Part II: The Long-Term Impact

Author's Note: *An excellent book to better understand the long-term effects of trauma and abuse on the body, mind, emotions, and spirit is* The Body Keeps the Score *by Bessel van der Kolk.*

I walk up to the next available teller at my bank, someone I do not recognize. Tellers come and go, but I have come to know those who have remained for some time. He greets me with a warm smile and asks, "How can I help you?"

Smiling back, I reply, "I'm here to make a deposit," handing the checks and cash to him across the cold marble countertop. He politely says, "Ma'am, you must have a deposit slip. I can give you one to fill out."

My calm, kind, but clarifying response to him is, "No, I know that I no longer need to use a deposit slip here at my bank. You can deposit this straight into my business account."

He makes eye contact with me and is no longer smiling. His jaw has sternly set, and his reaction is clear and emphatic. "No, that is not the case here. You must have a deposit slip."

My stomach tightens and my teeth clench, a visceral reaction to this challenge. This kid is telling me that I have no idea what I am talking about. I have been banking here for years, and people know me. I look around but realize that I see not even one familiar face. For a split second, I flash to the image of Rod Serling saying, "Next stop, the Twilight Zone."

What is currently unfolding, however, is not funny. I tense up and reiterate, "I have been a customer at this bank for decades; I *know* that I no longer need a deposit slip. I have more than one account here. Just look it up and deposit these checks into the business account."

He is obviously perturbed, his face now flushed. He reaches for a deposit slip to pass over to me, leaving it on my side of the two-way impasse.

I grab it, feeling real anger building within me as my words come out sarcastically, "Fine! I will fill out the deposit slip because you don't know that there is no need for this." My comment is loud enough to grab the attention of a manager, because she makes her way over to our counter. I observe that she is not one of the managers that I know, now even more aware that I am in the bank with all strangers.

"Is there a problem here?" she asks politely, using her managerial-customer-care voice.

"Yes, there is a problem here," I reply, relieved. "I have been banking here for years, and I have not had to fill out a deposit slip since the policy changed. He," I say as I halfway glance toward the teller, "has been emphatic that I *must* fill one out. People know me here at the bank, and they simply put my deposit straight into my business account."

The manager takes a step back from the counter, her face now flushed, and using a snide and authoritative tone, she says, "Well, *I* don't know you."

Her reply is the final bomb to my ability to find any lingering resources of calm.

"That is not my problem!" I snap back at her, feeling my blood pressure skyrocketing. "I have my bank ID card, the account numbers, and I have *never* needed a deposit slip. It is possible to make a deposit without a deposit slip!"

She turns to the teller and says, "She is right. It is possible to deposit without a deposit slip, but I see that you were not shown how to do this." She proceeds to show him how to enter it into the computer and process the cash and checks directly into my account.

I stand there stunned. *Seriously?* Now *she admits to the teller and everyone in the bank that I know what the hell I am talking about?* I want to react, but I remain quiet, my nerves still quivering as I attempt to refocus back to the current reality.

I have no recall of what happened next, other than that niceties were shared. I sense the teller is not happy, as he's making no eye contact with me. I begin to feel a little, tiny bit sorry for him, because I know how it feels to be humbled in public.

I leave the bank feeling frustrated, embarrassed, and depleted. *Why did I react the way that I did? This is not like me. My patience and kindness were blown into oblivion.* In this encounter with the teller, I became the person that I myself have often found intolerable. *Why did my self-control disappear? What triggered me into this unacceptable reaction?*

I get into my car and start to cry. A barrage of ugly names for myself fills my head, in addition to all the feelings that are erupting within me. In this moment, life itself feels like too much to handle. I just need to get home.

I lie in bed, my ear throbbing with the familiar pain of another ear infection. I have cried through many nights with no relief from the pain, and now I hear my dad calling the doctor to come to the parsonage. This means that I am going to get a penicillin shot. I am too young to understand that the pain from the shot will heal the excruciating pain in my ears.

As an older child and into my teens, strep throat was an ongoing occurrence in all four seasons, and I encountered periodic ear infections into adulthood. Eventually, as an adult, I had tympanoplasty surgery done on my left eardrum. It had been perforated so many times that I was at risk of hearing loss. Even with this successful repair, ten years later I would again get an infection in my left ear, acquired during a short pool swim while on vacation. It took seven months of weekly visits to a highly skilled ENT to clear up that infection.

In junior high school, the track coach wanted me to join the track team. I was a fast runner and I loved to run, but whenever I ran, I would become ill. It would take three days to recover from the aches, muscle pains, painful lungs, and overall weakness I experienced.

When I turned sixty, I decided to start CrossFit. I thoroughly enjoyed both the physical challenge and the resultant strength I achieved. After several months of doing this, I felt affirmed in my newfound strength and fitness.

One day, however, I began to feel weak, achy, and overall not well. The more I did CrossFit, the sicker I became. After many months of tests, a specialist found an area in my immune system that registered exceptionally low. The cure for this, which I underwent for several months, was weekly infusions to replace what I was missing. I felt great with this treatment—until I suddenly reacted to it with a mild stroke. I was immediately taken off the treatment.

At one point, I was in so much pain that I feared that one day I might not be able to walk. Points of pain shot through my legs like blazing needles. Muscle spasms increased, generating excruciating pain that took up to twenty minutes to release. The way I compensated for my leg pain began to affect my lower back. Neurologists did their best to help me with injections and find the source of my pain, but nothing gave me relief and answers were not found.

Tess, my physical therapist, did everything she knew to do as a highly skilled physical therapist. She worked with the neurologists, prescribing the exercises they suggested, which only worsened my pain. It was not until my pain was understood to be related to fascia that I began to heal. Tess was patient and committed to find answers, working alongside my physician as they both suspected that the pain might be originating within the fascia. They were right. An area that is especially ignored and misunderstood is the physical impact of trauma to the fascia. Tess began working on this area, and slowly my legs were restored to full function.

In addition, the battle with weight gain and loss has dogged me throughout my adult life. The lie I believed was that I could "just do it" or have stronger willpower. This did not work.

There were the years of migraine headaches, seven or more sinus infections a year, allergies, and the need to learn to relax to overcome the impact that the daily (since childhood) dump of adrenaline had had on my body.

One by one, I took on each physical aliment and emotional trigger. I have eliminated most of the physical ailments. Some I have learned to live with and have been able to reduce their occurrence to a minimum. I rarely get ill now, but I do have to avoid getting overtired.

I owe my physical recovery to good medical care and emotional healing. The healthier I got emotionally, the healthier I became physically. I do not doubt that my vulnerability to various illnesses has had to do with what my body endured from the trauma and abuse I encountered as a child.

It is easy to dismiss how our bodies react by saying, "That's just the way it is." It is good to understand that our bodies do keep score of what has happened to us. Our amazing bodies are not made of iron, and part of healing is

The Destroyer, Part II: The Long-Term Impact

to show compassion for what our bodies have been through in life.

※

I enter the medical building with an unusual combination of anxiety and calm, a bit unsure what to expect. I have just been here a few weeks earlier to have my thyroid biopsied. On that last visit, I had a wonderful, kind doctor who performed the biopsy so skillfully that I experienced little discomfort. That had been on his last day, however, before moving his practice elsewhere.

At the end of that visit, this gentle doctor had told me that my report would be back within a week. The biopsy came back inconclusive, and so now I was back for a second biopsy. It could be cancer, and obviously I need to know.

I exit the elevator and walk down the hallway to the same office where I had previously been seen. I walk in and give my name to the receptionist, who tells me to take a seat and someone will be with me shortly.

A door opens, and a nurse calls my name. I follow her back to the familiar room. This somehow brings me some comfort—but I still wish I was seeing the same doctor because he had earned my confidence.

I despise my low tolerance and my fear of physical pain. *This new doctor had better be skilled*, I think.

The nurse leaves, and some minutes later the doctor comes in. Initially, his very presence causes me to pause. He stands six feet four, maybe five, inches tall, with muscular, broad shoulders and a take-charge demeanor. (I later found out he was a military-trained physician.) I feel more unsure about how this procedure will go.

I begin some reassuring self-talk in my head. *Faith, it will be okay. You did this before, and it went well. You know it will be over soon. Three needle draws and it will be over; then you can leave. Just breathe, relax, breathe.*

The doctor begins, "I'm Doctor So-and-so. Please lie back on the table and don't move—be as still as you can be."

As I do as I am told, the door opens and a new nurse comes in. I look over to my left to see her standing at a counter with her back to me. She remains positioned there the entire time of the procedure. She never speaks to me, looks at me, or connects with me throughout the entire biopsy. She is only there to take the samples.

The doctor positions my neck as I prepare myself to repeat what I had done just a few weeks prior. Standing behind me, he reiterates, "Stay very still and don't move."

The needle penetrates my skin and muscles. With this comes a surge of pain that shoots through my neck and into my body, unlike any pain I have ever felt. It is *not* like the last time I did this. My eyes tear up, but I do not move. I have a needle in my neck.

As if it was no big deal, the doctor removes the needle and says, "Oops, that one did not work. I will have to do this one over again."

I began to panic. *Seriously? I must do these three more times? Are they all going to be this painful? Does he know what he is doing?* I do everything I can to calm myself down and prepare for the next needle to enter my neck into my thyroid. I begin to feel myself moving into survival mode. I must get through this, and there is nothing I can do but survive what is happening to me.

I take a deep breath, realizing that the doctor has now moved from directly behind me to be more to my right side at my head. Before he inserts the needle into my neck, his arm comes down to rest on my breast. I freeze.

He removes the needle, handing it to the nurse as I lie frozen on the table, unsure of what I have just experienced. The pain was excruciating with his placement of the needle, and the placement of his arm on my breast has my brain spinning with fear and confusion. I still have two more injections to go.

The second needle goes in, and again, pain shoots through my neck. My thoughts are now smashing into each other. *Is he that inept, or is he doing this deliberately to me to cause me as much pain as possible?* I can't scream. I can't move. I must lie there perfectly still; he has all the control.

His arm again presses against my breast as the needle goes in and remains there until he withdraws it from my throat. With his exact previous motion, he hands the needle to the nurse who faces toward the counter and wall. *Why isn't she involved in what he is doing with me? Is this how he does things and she does not want to see, or has she been told not to see?*

One more to go. I tell myself I can do this. Taking an incredibly difficult breath, I prepare for the third injection. The third one is as painful as the first two as well as the "oops" injection. His arm lays on my breast one last time. I try to fix my mind on the fact that this is really happening, but my thoughts are numbed and fading. I find myself feeling frozen, afraid, and losing touch with my current surroundings.

I feel him remove the needle. A small wave of relief rolls over me, knowing that he is done. When the nurse receives the last needle from him, she turns and heads out of the room. I am now alone with this man.

I sit up at the end of the table, and the doctor walks over and positions himself at the bottom of the table, facing me. He is two to five inches away from me. He towers over me, and he does not remove his gaze. He does not smile or offer words of encouragement. His intimidating stance keeps me immobilized. *Just listen, nod, and get out of here*, I think.

This is exactly what I do. I have no idea what he says to me. Fear wraps around my chest like a tightening vice, and I begin to panic, afraid that I might pass out. I need to get away from this man and get to my car.

He finishes his words, turns, and leaves the room. I jump off the table, reach for my purse on the chair, and head out the door. Finding my way out of the office to the elevator, I head to the ground floor. I pick up my pace as I exit the doors. I find myself close to running to reach my car. Unlocking it, I slip into the driver's seat, quickly lock all the doors, and erupt into uncontrollable sobbing.

So many thoughts run through my mind about what has just happened. With my thoughts come a flood of emotions. I cannot sort any of it out. My tears and sobs are all I know.

The Destroyer, Part II: The Long-Term Impact

It takes some time to quiet myself enough to believe I can drive safely home. I begin to feel anger for freezing in that moment. I begin to judge myself for not speaking up, not stopping the procedure, and not telling him to get away from me. These were all the things I swore and believed I would do if anything like this ever happened. Instead, this unexpected encounter silenced me, froze me, and left me gripped with fear—feeling victimized yet again.

Why do I react this way? With all the healing that I have done over the years, how can this have been my response? Yes, I was triggered, but I have handled triggers before. Today I froze.

The trauma and abuse of my past left my spiritual beliefs in a morass of confusion. I had had two major influences occurring in my life at the same time, pulling me in opposite directions. I had been taught that God, a higher being, was good, yet I experienced at the hands of my abusers that the higher being was evil. My center of truth, meaning, and values left me to spin out of control one day and then quickly be yanked back to being fully in control another—or so I thought.

By the time I became a teenager, I had no idea what I believed anymore. My night terrors were horrific, my self-esteem below zero. Football jocks called me ugly in the classroom and yelled names at me down the hallway. I felt pulled into two different worlds—one that was good and one that was evil—yet neither held the answers I ached to find.

Through most of my early adult years I continued to carry shame, guilt, and fear, no matter which spiritual reality pulled me into its whirlpool. I was damned if I did and damned if I didn't.

By choosing performance to succeed, I found an exit door out of the heart-gripping agony I was experiencing. I could engage with people, succeed in business, and excel in whatever I set my mind to. I was living my life and finding out what had meaning and value to me. I even began to wrestle with the deeper meaning to life and spirituality.

What I had no way of knowing was that what had been embedded in my mind and body years before had not been erased by my success. The time was fast approaching when I would need to face my past. The choice was to face what had happened to me or ignore it by brushing it away with excuses and denial.

Somewhere deep inside me, I knew I had to turn inward and do the challenging work to overcome what had been restraining me from living freely.

So, I did the work. I overcame the monsters and the things that go bump in the night. During the process of facing my past, I often found myself relating to Bilbo Baggins's journey in J.R.R. Tolkien's novel *The Hobbit*. I, too, was called out of my daily routine where I had found safety and predictability, to be taken on a terrifying, exhilarating, and revolutionary journey that led me down a path to freedom and new life.

This phase of my journey was the hardest work I have ever done, yet I can honestly say that I do not regret the demand that was required of me. I am now free to live, no longer held and trapped by the horrors of my past.

And so I live, and I also continue to succeed in what I know I must do—to help other survivors of childhood abuse find their way into freedom. As I continue to heal and give back to those who need someone who understands what they have been through, my inner spirit settles. I find a truth to live by; I find peace; I find hope; I find purpose and meaning, and my spirituality is founded in love by the Author of love.

My spiritual beliefs are foundational to my ongoing journey in life. As it is with all aspects of becoming who I really am, I must face my inadequacies, mess-ups, doubts, and unkind responses toward others. Then I must ask myself, *Where did this arise from?* It is then that I show myself grace and understanding to be able to change, to correct, to seek forgiveness, and to offer love in place of the shortcomings of my false self.

When I offer love to myself and to others, I take back out of the hands of my abusers their power to define what I believe.

Reflection on My Story

It is unimaginable that any human being would inflict evil horrors upon any child or adult, yet we read of this in the newspaper and hear of it on the evening news. As I moved through my recovery, facing the impact that Ted and others had on my life, I chose to walk through the many layers of trauma that had been stockpiled upon my soul—psyche, body, and spirit.

The brunt force of abuse that I met as a child led to a ripple effect of aftershocks in my life. Once I entered the recovery phase, I began to understand why I believed or behaved in ways that were destructive to me. But this discovery was only the beginning. There was so much more for me to discover—to understand, to process, and to connect the dots of why, after facing the demons in my life, I could still become reactionary when I least expected it.

My Bank Experience: I reacted to the teller because I was not heard and believed, and my input was dismissed by being told that I did not know what I was talking about. I felt humiliated by the teller and manager. It may have been my perception in the moment or a combination of the teller's and the manager's body language and dismissive tone. Whatever the truth of the experience, I was triggered with a flood of shame and humiliation, which were the tools often used by my abusers. My reaction was out of line. In that moment, I was unable to be the person I know myself to be.

The Impact on the Body: There has been a great deal of research done on how trauma affects the body and mind. I have suffered ongoing physical effects from the blows of the trauma I experienced, and I have been determined to heal and reclaim my body and mind. Investing into this part of recovery was every bit as important as investing into my emotional recovery.

My Doctor Experience: When I froze and could not react in the way I assumed I would in a situation like this, I had feelings of guilt, shame, and humiliation—along with the old feelings of powerlessness. What I knew—even though it made no difference while the event was happening—was that I had an automatic programmed response to "freeze," developed to help me survive. Several triggers on that day caused this automatic response.

The Impact on Spirituality: A controlling version of spirituality attempted to rob me of a good spirituality that could center and offer me deeper meaning. Working through this negative spirituality became a part of my journey where I would find spiritual truth.

I have often used the analogy that abuse is a major, life-shattering earthquake with many powerful aftershocks. However, it is the unexpected tsunami of long-term effects that carries with it a different level of destruction that then must be explored and understood. I thought that by cleaning up the destruction of the emotional earthquake in my life, I was done—until my tsunami hit. Truth be told, you cannot clean up what has not yet happened.

I now live in the reality of both/and. I have overcome incredible things in my life in order to be at peace with my existence and to love God, others, and my true self. And being fully aware that I am fallible, I can still have physical or emotional triggers that I must own and deal with. All my blunders and failings remain an opportunity for me to explore and transform, thus allowing me to continue to evolve into my authentic self.

What Is Your Story?

Have you noticed or ever wondered if your health is connected in any way to the circumstances you have been through?

Have you stopped to wonder why you react to certain situations in ways that you later regret?

Have you tossed aside, minimized, or avoided spirituality because of a negative experience you had with it?

Have you ever found yourself in a fight-flight-or-freeze situation, where you had no idea why you reacted the way that you did?

Share Your Story

Giving voice to your story aids in releasing the power it may still have in your life.

Who is the person you believe you could share your story with?

What is currently most concerning to you? Your body, your mind, your emotions, your spirituality? Whatever is currently happening in that area of your life, can you take the risk and share this with someone you trust?

The Destroyer, Part II: The Long-Term Impact

Believe you are worth it to tell someone what is going on in your life, because you are.

12

Treasure Found

Sitting across from Kinsley, who is obviously in deep emotional pain, I listen intently as she shares her life story with me. I hear the devastating effect that the invasion of the "thief" had on her life. This "thief" is all of the circumstances that have stolen her confidence, her voice, and her ability to see herself for who she really is. It had also robbed her of her love for life, her joy, and her purpose. It has made her believe that she does not have the right to live a full and productive life.

All that the thief has stolen from her has left a void that has cultivated doubt, silence, lies, hate, depression, a loss of vision for her life. She has felt a monumental hopelessness that life could ever be different from what she is experiencing in this very moment.

She weeps as she shares details that have wounded her heart. A less-than-nurturing mother who was caught up in herself, a father who was rarely home, an abusive babysitter, cruel kids at school who made fun of her speech impediment, boys who used her sexually in high school, as she mistakenly believed that being wanted would replace the pain of rejection that continually tormented her.

More individuals robbed her in college and at her place of employment. Finally, she would marry an emotionally abusive husband whom she would find the courage to leave, only to return to him—leave again and then return—multiple times over during the last decade.

Kinsley suddenly exclaims, "I have NO value! My life has no value! I am worthless! I cannot live this way anymore—I don't *want* to live anymore."

She is one of the hundreds, and by now thousands, of individuals whose stories I have listened to over the last thirty-eight years, both men and women. Although the stories I've listened to have similarities, every one of them is unique to the person telling them. Their pain and suffering are exclusive; their torment is singular; the hopelessness that fills their hearts is unequaled to anyone else's experience, because it is theirs alone to feel and to withstand.

I listen and feel deep compassion for Kinsley. The details she has shared needed to be heard.

When Kinsley can quiet herself, with tears still streaming down her face, I speak in as gentle of a voice as I can offer her.

"Kinsley, I would like to share something with you, if you would like me to."

Kinsley nods yes.

I continue, "Kinsley, take in some deep breaths. Right now, you are not breathing normally, your breathing is shallow, and your body and brain need a healthy refueling of oxygen. I will breathe with you."

I begin to inhale through my nose and exhale through my mouth, each breath slow, steady, and deepening. Kinsley begins to mirror me. In a few minutes, Kinsley becomes calmer and more alert. *One more thing the thief steals*, I think—*even our ability to take a deep breath when we need it most.*

"Kinsley, I want to share an analogy that came to me some years ago. Can I share this with you now?" Again, Kinsley nods to proceed.

"I saw a photo of the Hope Diamond in a magazine article I happened to pick up. I was in awe of it. The size of it, the beauty of it. So many people over time have sought to claim it as their own. To this day, it is considered priceless.

"I want you to imagine with me that you and I are outside on my driveway. The Hope Diamond is being brought up the driveway to us by armored guards. They take it from the armored van, bring it to us, and place it first in my hands. I look it over carefully, and then I place it into your hands. You feel the weight of it; you see its brilliance and how the sunlight reflects off it.

"There are no words to express its magnificence.

"I then ask you to place it on the pavement.

"You cannot imagine degrading this jewel in such a way, but reluctantly you do it. You place it ever so gently on the tar-blackened path. Just as you do this, we both hear a truck backing up, *beep ... beep ... beep ...* as it descends my driveway. The dump truck nears the Hope Diamond, stopping within inches of it.

"It is now close enough that we can smell what is loaded in the truck: warm, steaming, fresh manure. We hear the hydraulics move into action as the back of the loader lifts upward. It stops at an angle that begins to deliver its load onto this cherished jewel. Hundreds of pounds of stinky excrement cover it. Within minutes, the dumping is complete. The driver returns to the cab and drives away.

"We are left standing there, seeing and smelling this massive pile of pollutants, yet fully aware that beneath all this dung lies the priceless ... Hope ... Diamond.

"Has the Hope Diamond lost its value?" I ask Kinsley.

After a long stretch of silence Kinsley replies, "No, it has not lost its value."

"You're right—you are *absolutely* right," I respond. "The Hope Diamond has not lost its value, but its value and its beauty must be found again. Its incalculable value cannot be discarded. The only way you will find it is to dig into the mound of manure and reclaim it. Once found, you will wash it off and return it to its rightful place for the world to see.

"Kinsley, this is exactly what you are doing on your courageous journey: facing head-on and healing the many things that never should have happened to you. You chose to venture into this unknown to overcome the obstacles that have impacted your life. It makes perfect sense to me that, as painful as the spot is that you are currently in, you just want the suffering to end.

"But hear me—really hear me. You are like the Hope Diamond that will shine. But first you must find your true value that lies beneath all the lies, hurt, betrayals, cruelty, and rejection that you have endured.

"What are you likely to discover?

"The truth, your voice, and your way to live out your life as the woman you were designed to be.

"You can do this, Kinsley, because you have already come so far. You are aware that there is more to life than what you could have ever imagined. Do not give up now. You have fought hard to get to where you currently are, and there is more to come. Where you are now is not your end but a passageway to where you are going. And I believe you will navigate this phase of your expedition well.

"Remember, you are not on this journey alone. You have good people who care about you and will support you—even on your most difficult of days."

Kinsley's story holds elements of my own story. My circumstances were different from hers, but I was able to relate to her experience.

In life, it is a given that I will go through times of pain, loss, rejection, disappointment, and even being violated. I am a human being, and difficult, painful times are inevitable. My own times of adversity absolutely knocked me flat on my face—just as the times of blessing raised me to my feet. As I have stated so often, "Life is not either/or; life is both/and."

How quickly I wanted to avoid, move on, or numb out the darker times in my life, yearning to experience more pleasant things. But oh, what I would have missed by ignoring, rushing past, or covering up whatever I dreaded facing. This would have been an added tragedy.

I discovered that what rests between the layers of my pain, hopelessness, and struggles are nuggets of gold: wisdom, knowledge, truth, and breakthrough. During my darkest hours, I came to understand what I had not seen about myself, others, and my circumstances. As hard as it has been to face what I would have rather bypassed, I found peace in releasing my tears and fears. I found an abundance of treasure by embracing all of life.

Who I have become and am becoming would not have happened if I had pushed aside the darkest nights of my soul.

Indeed, I love the good days and hope I can avoid the ones that I end up calling "bad days." However, the truth is, nothing that has happened to me or that I have chosen to do—positive or negative—is wasted. When I allow it, each of my experiences has taught me, guided me, revealed the truth to me, healed me, matured me, and influenced me to become the person who will better my life and hopefully the lives of others.

I cannot change the past and what has happened, but an added setback would have been if I missed discovering the good that is to be found among the ashes. When I choose to face my nightmares head-on, the goal is to overcome them and move on into a more fulfilling way of life. Yet this can only happen when I listen to what my nightmares reveal—the deeper hidden truths I have knowingly, and unknowingly, sought to avoid.

It was while I was dealing with an internal struggle in writing this closing chapter that I had a dream that revealed to me a significant connection that I had yet to make. My dream's message revealed all I had lost throughout my life and my sadness over what could have been. I had worked through my layers of grief, but there remained a missing piece for me to do. I was not *honoring* what I had lost.

I realized I needed to memorialize and lay to rest what had been taken from me over the course of my life.

Before I could write about the treasures I found, I needed to hear the message embedded within my dream. That message: *You cannot celebrate the Treasure Found until you honor what you have lost.* The pain I felt in the dream now made sense to me. My subconscious had worked overtime to reveal that there was a step I must take before attending my victory party.

I can relate this awareness to a pet peeve I have. It deeply bothers me when people plan a "celebration of life" style memorial service before having had a service of grief for those who remain hurt, feeling their all-consuming loss for their loved one. I have always believed that both services are required. Each has immense value in the healing of broken hearts, but all too often, the service of grief is bypassed when someone we love is no longer with us. Too often, we want to avoid our pain and just move on.

My dream brought to the surface a layer of heartbreak that I had not known was there.

I entered a space of bereavement as I began to weep over the images of my past that ran through my mind. I cried as I shared my dream with my husband and later with my therapist, Rich. I allowed deep sobs to shatter a dam that held back a lifetime of loss, grief, pain, and heartbreak. Although I had allowed the creeks and rivers of my sorrow to flow out over the years, I was unaware of a greater volume of grief that still needed release. I recovered, exhausted but lighter, feeling freer and at peace.

My mental and emotional vision came into focus. I turned and looked behind me and saw my past fading in the distance, while at the same time an unexplored territory was opening and expanding before me . . . my future.

When it seemed impossible for me to believe that there was anything of worth about me, there remained an element of truth that propelled me forward to dig and not give up. After digging through the pile of emotional manure that others, including myself, had placed on me, I found it! There it was. Bright, shining, glorious, priceless, exquisite, radiant, and full of hope.

I found me.

My true, authentic, original self.

THE TREASURES I HAVE FOUND

Buried beneath the pile and weight of . . .

- . . . lies, I found truth.
- . . . shame, I found honor and self-respect.
- . . . fear, I found confidence and contentment.
- . . . anger, I found calmness, kindness, and goodwill.
- . . . resentments, I found empathy, sympathy, and rapport.
- . . . hate, I found love, respect, and blessing.
- . . . secrecy, I found honesty, openness, and being known.
- . . . prejudice, I found tolerance, fairness, and fondness.
- . . . silence, I found permission granted to speak and release.
- . . . rejection, I found admission, acknowledgment, and self-acceptance.
- . . . panic, I found courage and self-assurance.
- . . . intimidation, I found empowerment and boundaries.
- . . . defensiveness, I found vulnerability, openness, and pause.
- . . . anxiety, I found tranquility, breathing, and a slower pace.
- . . . neglect, I found self-care, music for my soul, and rest.
- . . . my past, I found my future.

When I found my treasure, I needed to carefully steward and examine each gem of truth. It takes time to reflect on the value and purpose of each. I've spent time meditating on how each gem I found would change me. I am continually learning their value and how they are each meant to be applied to my life. I have much to learn, but this is all part of my ongoing adventure.

I close this chapter by sharing with you a few of my experiences on how individual gems have changed my life.

For most of my life, I reacted vehemently when anything negative or painful came my way. I found myself getting angry, "Why me? It's not fair!" I would blame others or myself with harsh judgments. When life got disrupted by disappointment or suffering, I resented this change from the safety I had created. It terrified me.

I wanted quick fixes to what had been turned upside down. I wanted it to be put right side up—immediately! I had a great deal to heal to discover where these extreme reactions came from. I did the work, and these two gems have altered how I respond to change.

> *GEM #1: Change is a part of life that does not need to be feared. Change means that something is happening. I can fight it, assuming that there is no good to be found in this transition. Or I can embrace it and discover its value. How I choose to move through this time will influence the outcome, because I have a major part in creating the ways in which I want life to be different.*

> **GEM #2: Just when I feel or believe that life will never change, it will.**

This next story shows how I discovered the third gem that I am meant to think for myself.

In 1960, two men ran to become president of the United States: Richard M. Nixon and John F. Kennedy, who was a Catholic. My dad was genuinely concerned that a Catholic might become president—so much so that he managed the Republican headquarters in our town. Since he was one of the local pastors, I am not sure how the separation of church and state played into this. However, his conviction was so strong that Kennedy should be defeated that he did what he believed he had to do.

At the age of ten, I was fascinated with the balloons, streamers, and large posters of Nixon and his running partner, Lodge, that hung in the window of the Republican headquarters. But what mostly enticed me were the donuts. The delicious bakery delights were always set out to draw people into the headquarters to pick up brochures and chat over coffee and a donut.

Main Street was near to our parsonage, and I would run down to spend time standing for a candidate that my dad believed in. I knew my dad wanted as many people as possible to see it his way as well.

The truth is, as much as I liked the donuts, I disliked the poster of Nixon. He was creepy to me, scary. Even at the age of ten, something inside me did not trust him.

One day, I walked farther down Main Street to the storefront where posters of Kennedy were hanging in the window. I looked inside and saw the same type of set up. Balloons, streamers, tables with brochures, and people having coffee and donuts. I stood for some time looking at the face of Kennedy. I felt comfort and peace from his face.

When Kennedy won that year, my dad was distraught. He dismantled Nixon's headquarters and went on with life. His fear that the Pope would take over our country never happened.

I was taught to be a Republican, so for many years I never gave it a second thought. At the age of nineteen, I married an ultraconservative Republican who had been in Young Republicans as a leader. So it continued. My parents taught me to think that what they said was right. I married a man who said that thinking one way—his way—was right, and I followed.

When Nixon was caught for his crimes and resigned, I felt relief. I had been correct at the age of ten—he was not trustworthy or safe.

It took me many years to begin to figure out that I could think for myself about which candidate I thought would best serve our country. I switched parties and became a Democrat, but found that I did not always fall in line with all their policies. Then one day it *finally* occurred to me that I could vote as an Independent. This freed me to discern and decide for myself who I thought might best serve our country at any given time. When I became a voter who voted for *my* choice, I found my political voice. Now, my vote *really* matters.

> **GEM #3: Think for myself. Weigh everything with the wisdom I've cultivated over the years. My voice and my choice matter.**

For many years I have had people tell me I needed to write a book. I would smile and say things like, "Maybe one day," or "I'm not sure about that." I recall most often saying, "I'm not a writer." The truth was, I was terrified to author a book. I had a long-held fear that I would fail; and what would I write about anyway?

I knew nothing about the reality of becoming an author and navigating the details to bring a book to life. I was unaware that there are proficient people to help with this. My guess is that it was mostly fear of rejection from readers that kept me from starting the process. Yet among the treasures I've found, I grabbed hold of this one and authored this book, *Treasure Found*.

> **GEM #4: All new challenges are opportunities to grow and develop as a person. In the end, there are gems to be found: triumph, fulfillment, achievement, and self-actualization.**

As I mentioned earlier, I was pulled in opposite directions as to what to believe. Seeking what resonates as spiritually significant is a personal journey. What I found for my life has been healing and supportive, transformational and grounding, purposeful and good. Here is what I found.

God is for me, not against me. God loves me in a way that is kind, generous, and patient, offering all that is good to me. God is a friend who is always with me, and is far more than what my finite brain can comprehend. It is not my place to define God, but I can embrace what I have come to understand and experience about God. God is not a religion, nor does God side with a political affiliation. God is relational and seeks relationship by continually offering grace, forgiveness, and transformation without punishment or cruel judgment. God faithfully walks with me through the most painful and the most joyous of days. God is not like the humans I have known. God is good, and God is life—not death. God is Love.

After several years of sifting through the confusion, anger, frustration, and false expectations I had about God, I ventured into an incredible part of my journey where I began to discover for myself what God is all about. It became a six-year quest for me. I needed to find the answer for myself: the truth about God and God's true character. I did not take this venture lightly. I allowed time to unfold what my heart was seeking to encounter and what my mind longed to understand.

What a powerful and engaging pilgrimage it was. This time in my life was filled with stories that could form another book. I have many journals documenting my experiences, and I treasure the memories that they hold. I began to listen to other voices that varied from the ones I had been raised on. Morton Kelsey's book, *The Other Side of Silence*, impacted my life and thinking. I dove into more of his writing as well as that of other authors who broadened my perspective.

I wrestled honestly and got both angry and real with God. God revealed to me divine patience and tenderness with each round of outbursts.

Next, I began to take God out of my box, including the box that so much of my religious teaching had placed God in. This was terrifying for me, because what if I was wrong? Would God punish me?

The next part of my journey was to discover if God was or wasn't out to "get me." What I discovered is that God only desires to offer me the truth about who God is.

The interesting outcome was this: I did not need to throw the baby out with the bathwater. Not all that I had been taught was off base. The ultimate Teacher was spot-on, however. It is this Teacher who led me to see the truth about God, which is so much more than I could ever have comprehended. He exemplifies God in every way.

I was a lot like one of Jesus's followers, Phillip, at the beginning of my quest:

> Philip said, "Master, show us the Father; then we'll be content."

[Jesus replied,] "You've been with me all this time, Philip, and you still don't understand? To see me is to see the Father. So how can you ask, 'Where is the Father?' Don't you believe that I am in the Father and the Father is in me? The words that I speak to you aren't mere words. I don't just make them up on my own. The Father who resides in me crafts each word into a divine act.

"Believe me: I am in my Father and my Father is in me. If you can't believe that, believe what you see—these works. (John 14:8–14 MSG)

I began to really study to see the life and character of Jesus. I came to know for myself that I could trust the teachings of Jesus and who He was. I chose to align myself spiritually with Jesus, because His teachings are sound and represent a life that I want to live. I want to be honest, safe, caring, compassionate, giving, generous, loving, forgiving toward all, open, accepting, and patient. Jesus advocated for the abused and so much more. Jesus' life exemplified all this to me. He said, "To see me is to see the Father"—i.e., God.

Believing in something greater than myself was, and continues to be, invaluable on this expedition of life. Especially on my most painful and difficult days, it has been beneficial to have more than just myself to trust in.

Whatever your belief might be—even if you do not believe in anything spiritually—one thing I would encourage is that you must know, really *know*, why you do or don't believe as you do. This is the integrity and honesty that you offer to yourself and to others.

> *GEM #5: My spiritual faith centers me, continues to transform me, gives me comfort, support, and direction for my existence. It prepares me for the life before me.*

> *GEM #6: Grace is by far the greatest treasure of all, because without grace, I would easily fall back into self-condemnation, people pleasing, and perfectionism. The less weight I carry, the lighter and freer I will be.*

Each gem I have found has been life-changing for me. I will continue to learn how to apply each of these treasures to my life. I will fail at times, for I am imperfect. But as I allow each gem to be absorbed into my DNA, over time I will become a reflection of each valuable treasure found.

Final Word to My Readers

C. S. Lewis said, "You can't go back and change the beginning, but you can start where you are and change the ending."

C. S. Lewis spoke the truth: you hold the power to change your ending by beginning your own personal expedition.

Wherever your journey takes you, how you deal with life's inevitable ups and downs will depend on how you respond now.

Your past cannot define you unless you choose to do nothing about it. You have been given an incredible opportunity—a gift—to change the ending of your story by becoming the person you seek to become.

The greatest treasure you will ever find is your authentic, true self. Herein lies your treasure to be found.

It will require you to commit to a lifelong journey, not a quick fix, nor a pick-up-the-answer-at-a-drive-through solution.

Facing what you would rather avoid will be scary at times, but I assure you that courage will rise within you.

There will be times you will want to forget it and revert to how you have previously dealt with life.

Hang in there. The painful and difficult times are temporary.

You do not need to do life on your own. There are those who will journey with you and even carry you when you need it. Be vulnerable and risk opening yourself up to receive what you need when you need it.

Celebrate the gems that you will be given along the way: breakthroughs, insights, discoveries, healing, and transformation. These are the building blocks of your new life and of the ending that is being magnificently formed.

Finally, you currently hold an amazing gift—your story. It is filled with truth and purpose for your life. Don't hide it, but share it. Freedom and wisdom exist within your story. These are two of the most valuable gems you will ever find.

The impossible is possible. I have shared this truth by sharing my story with you.

Now, what's your story?

Acknowledgments

These stories did not evolve all on their own. Along the way, I was encouraged, guided, and supported in ways that at the time were not always clear to me. These individuals each offered me something that became a stepping stone on my journey.

Looking back, I see the many gifts that came my way through kind people who offered what I needed, right when I needed it most. Each person laid a cobblestone for me to place my foot upon. Their goodness offered me the courage to take the next step before me.

Some encounters were momentary, some short-term, some prolonged, but each offered significant insight, wisdom, compassion, and guidance on my journey. Most have no idea of their impact on my life.

Some gifts were given via a passing sentence that awakened a truth within me. Some were a silent affirmation or words from an author that changed the course of my life by offering me a new thought. There were those who intervened on my behalf, counseled, guided, and challenged me. Every single one has played an invaluable role in my life and story.

There is, of course, a story I could write on each person and how our paths crossed. For now, I look to each individual with immense gratitude for the part they played in my life's journey. I recognize each unique gentleperson with my deepest appreciation. They were, and some continue to be, a key contributor in my life, to whom I will be forever grateful.

Brandon Addison – Life Coach
Richard Audsley – Marriage and Family Therapist, PhD, LMFT
Allison Bown – Speaker, Author, Friend
Rev. Donald Brust – Minister (Retired)
Robert Chinisci – PhD, Neuropsychologist
Howard Coker – PhD, Professor of Chemistry
Graham Cooke – Author, Speaker
Swami G
Arve Grimsmo – BA of Mortuary Science
Jean Grimsmo – Friend
Lois Melkonian – Master Certified Coach, Former Podcast Partner, Friend
Morton Kelsey – Author, Speaker, Professor, Psychologist, Episcopalian Priest
Ruth Peterson – Friend (Stand-in Grandmother)
Dick Savidge – MA of Divinity, MA of Arts, Marriage and Family Counseling
Rev. Orin Scandrett – Methodist Minister, Counselor, Twin Cities Habitat, Marathon Runner
Jonathan Sheldon – MD
Tess Steele – PT, DPT, IDN
The man in the fedora hat

Acknowledgments

Rev. Teri Todd – Methodist Minister Pastor (Retired), Friend
Asa Wood – Financial Wholesaler (Son-in-Law)
Paul Young – Author, Speaker

Special Acknowledgments

This book would not exist if not for four incredible influences in my life. They read each chapter as I wrote it and not only offered their encouragement but expressed their optimism, trust, and confidence in me along the way.

Meg Mittelstedt, my book coach and editor. You valiantly molded and encouraged my novice ability to write my first book. With genuine patience and a tender spirit, you helped me develop as a writer through your teaching and guidance. You saw something in me that I did not see in myself. Meg, for all that you so graciously offered me, I am abundantly grateful to you.

Rich Audsley, my therapist. Rich, one of your best insights into my life was when you said to me, "You need to write your book and find your voice." You were correct. My voice now resonates throughout the pages of this book—and I will continue to develop it throughout my life. Thank you, Rich, for speaking your observant truth. It has made a difference in my journey.

Allison Bown, my friend. You saw my early days of writing years ago and enthusiastically inspired me to keep writing, with the advice that fewer words are best. Your skill as an author validated that I did have something to say as a storyteller. Your tears and laughter over my words have blessed me to venture onward. I will always hear your voice in my mind telling me, "What you have to say will speak to others." Thank you, Allison, for believing in me.

David Donaldson, my husband. You stood with me as I set off on this next phase of my expedition to become an author. You reflectively read every word I wrote, and rewrote, and offered minimal comments in supporting my process—allowing me to find my own way. Yet when you shared your wisdom, it gave me pause to weigh your insight and to integrate your comments in clarifying my story. Your love, patience, and belief in me have been the light that helped me push away the darkness. I will love you forever.

Further Resources

FINDING A THERAPIST WHO FITS FOR YOU

When looking for a therapist to fit your needs, here are some things to know and to consider.

1. There is a therapist out there who will work well for you. If one does not fit, move on to another.
2. If a family member or close friend has a therapist who has helped them, this can be a good referral. Give that therapist a try.
3. Decide if you would feel more comfortable seeing a male or female therapist.

THE SEARCH MADE EASY

1. Go to www.psychologytoday.com.
2. Click on "Find a Therapist."
3. Type in your city/town and state.
4. You will find a list of therapists in your area.
5. Narrow your search by clicking on issues, insurance (even Medicare/Medicaid), gender, types, and more. You will find that you can focus your exact needs and find a therapist who is trained in these specific areas. This includes being trained in emotionally focused therapy (EFT), EMDR, cognitive behavioral

therapy (CBT), addictions, PTSD, trauma, abuse, couples therapy, family therapy, group therapy, religious needs, sexual issues, etc.

6. Therapists with training in emotionally focused therapy, Internal Family Systems therapy, and EMDR therapy are often able to walk their clients through their healing process with skill and compassion. This is not to say that there aren't other therapists using a different modality who are equally compassionate in their approach. It is up to you to find the therapist whose personality aligns with what *you* are needing.
7. Once you have narrowed your search, you will see a bio on each therapist, often with their website as well.
8. Place a call to those you are most interested in. Most therapists will offer a fifteen-to-thirty-minute call to hear what you are looking for and to answer your questions. Others will offer a brief call offering basic information.
9. Listen to what you sense in your initial contact. If you feel a connection with one or more of the therapists, set up an initial appointment.
10. When you get the sense that one of them is a "fit" for you, continue to see this therapist. If at any time you feel that something is not quite working for you, discuss this with your therapist. This may very well be an opportunity to find your voice and figure out what isn't working. You and your therapist can consider if you need to find a therapist trained specifically for your needs.

WHEN YOU NEED IMMEDIATE HELP OR NEED TO TALK TO SOMEONE AVAILABLE 24/7

National Sexual Assault Hotline: 1-800-656-4673
(For women, men, girls, boys, and teens)

Domestic and Dating Violence: 1-800-799-SAFE or 1-800-799-7233

National Center for Victims of Crime: 1-885-484-2846

National Human Trafficking Hotline: 1-888-373-7888
Text: 233733

National Center for Missing and Exploited Children: 1-800-843-5678

National Deaf Domestic Violence Hotline: 1-885-812-1001 (video call)

National Alliance on Mental Illness (NAMI): 1-800-950-6264

Suicide Hotline 24/7: 988 or 1-800-273-8255

BOOKS ON TRAUMA

There is a large selection of books available today written by professionals on healing, abuse, trauma, and other life issues. If you have a certain area of need, someone has likely written a book on it. Go to a bookstore and skim through some of the books you are interested in. Better yet, go to your local library and check out the ones that resonate with you.

Here are a couple of authors to consider reading:

BESSEL A. VAN DER KOLK

I suggest any of the following books authored by Dr. van der Kolk. He has researched extensively the issues around trauma and its impact on the body, mind, and emotions. His caring and kind approach toward those who suffer from trauma is evident in his writing.

- *The Body Keeps the Score: Brain, Mind, and Body in the Healing of Trauma*
- *Traumatic Stress: The Effects of Overwhelming Experience on Mind, Body, and Society*
- *Psychological Trauma*

PETER LEVINE, PH.D.

- *Healing Trauma: A Pioneering Program for Restoring the Wisdom of Your Body*

BOOKS ON SEXUAL ABUSE

- *Not Child's Play: An Anthology of Brother-Sister Incest*, edited by Risa Shaw
- *Spilled Milk*, by K.L. Randis

- *The Courage to Heal: A Guide for Women Survivors of Child Sexual Abuse*, by Ellen Bass and Laura Davis
- *The Courage to Heal Workbook*, by Laura Davis
- *Betrayed as Boys: Psychodynamic Treatment of Sexually Abused Men*, by Richard B. Gartner
- *Healing Sexually Betrayed Men and Boys: Treatment for Sexual Abuse, Assault, and Trauma*, by Richard B. Gartner
- *The Rape Recovery Handbook: Step-by-Step help for Survivors of Sexual Assault*, by Aphrodite Matsakis

BOOKS ON TREATMENT TECHNIQUES IN THERAPY

- **EMDR – Eye Movement Desensitization Reprocessing**
  - *Getting Past Your Past: Take Control of Your Life with Self-Help Techniques from EMDR Therapy*, by Francine Shapiro
  - *Eye Movement Desensitization and Reprocessing Therapy: Basic Principles, Protocols, and Procedures*, by Francine Shapiro
- **EFT – Emotionally Focused Therapy**
  - *Attachment Theory in Practice: Emotionally Focused Therapy (EFT) with Individuals, Couples, and Families*, by Susan M. Johnson

- **IFS – Internal Family Systems**
    - *Introduction to Internal Family Systems,* by Richard Schwartz
    - *Altogether You: Experiencing Personal and Spiritual Transformation with Internal Family Systems Therapy,* by Jenna Riemersma

About the Author

Faith Donaldson is a wife, mother of three daughters, and grandmother of eight. A former entrepreneur for twenty-threeyears, she switched hats to walk alongside hundreds of adult survivors of childhood abuse for the last thirty-two years as an unlicensed psychotherapist.

Visit her website at: www.authorfaithdonaldson.com.

Printed in the USA
CPSIA information can be obtained
at www.ICGtesting.com
LVHW041420280624
784154LV00006BA/965